A Spider in the Corner of my Mind

RICHARD J. CRONBORG

A SPIDER IN THE CORNER OF MY MIND

SHORT STORIES AND SOCIOLOGICAL OBSERVATIONS

2008

A Spider in the Corner of my Mind

ACKNOWLEDGMENTS

Thanks to my dear wife and daughter, for supporting my efforts in this endeavor. They endured the 'dark side' of me for years...Now I get the chance to show them how much I truly love them. Usually the best way for me to accomplish a feat of this magnitude is to merely keep my mouth shut, and give them hugs and love whenever they are in my presence. I have learned over the years that the best road to contentment in life is to go with the flow, a practice which is easier said than done. To my readers, I also owe many thanks. My first book, "The Journey", which is available through my publisher Booksurge.com, or on Amazon.com, has been quite a therapeutic experience for me. All my creative friends in the art world, and in my writers' groups, have added much needed knowledge to my creative processes. This book is dedicated to my daughter and her fiancé. I am wishing them a life filled with joy and happiness! The future looks bright for me. I hope to savor watching my grandchildren growing up, becoming fine individuals like their parents. I also hope my new son-in-law doesn't mind me turning his children into Chicago White Sox fans! Many thanks to Chuck Moesch, who did the photography and art work for the book covers, and to Patrick Mundschau, my editor, who continues to amaze me with his knowledge and willingness to help me with my various projects. I also want to thank my friend, C.P Kaestner, a man of many talents: Writer, artist, poet, skateboard designer, and all around renaissance man.

PROLOGUE

They Wi-Fi, I Hi-Fi...They Game-Boy...I am annoyed. Hey! Let's get all get connected! In modern society, we are inundated with cell phones, web-cams, electric brooms, anime cartoons, and ipods. Wealthy, white, suburban teenaged males are talking shit, and wearing bill caps on their heads cocked sideways. Baggy slacks are falling off their chicken asses, exposing Tommy Hilfiger boxer shorts...Screw them!... They hype the hip-hop 'cultcha', while Daddy makes his bread from some Software Company or International Global Stock Portfolio. The American economic community is all falling apart now, anyway. Wait till the Corporate big boys find their magic kingdom is imploding, and the foreclosure signs are stuck on their manicured lawns. I want to 'bitch slap' all of them. Most of these fathers and sons know nothing of poverty. I wonder what African-Americans think about the aberrant cultural manifestation of white hip-hop culture, but I am afraid to ask. Many of our new age American youth refuse to wash dishes, deliver pizzas, cut grass, pick fruit, work on cars, labor in factories, or fix things that need fixing. They think that these jobs are beneath them. These jobs are for immigrants, blacks, and hillbillies. I say: "God bless the working man." My respect goes to any individual who isn't afraid of getting his hands dirty. He's 'made his bones,' paid his dues, and deserves a lot more than he gets from the new America. If Gus Hall wasn't dead, and on the ballot for the upcoming Presidential election, I'd vote for him. The kids don't look at me anymore, because I am a 'geezer'. Perchance, I am some grim reminder of what lies ahead for them. "They" rush through supermarkets, cutting me off. I try to stay out of their way. I promise myself to never use the self-checkout, because this act takes away a job from an American worker. It's ludicrous to me to be price-gouged, and to work for the grocery store at the same time. Where's my wages for checking myself out? This new ploy, is a Corporate insult to my intelligence. The television sets and cameras are everywhere, because they like to keep their eyes on us. We can't be trusted. "They" can google our backyards, and the Feds' probably have satellites up there in the skies, which can watch me have sex with my wife in the wrongly perceived privacy of my bedroom. What's next? "Get in the right hand lane, old fella'. That's alright by me. The automated, camera infested toll ways can take a picture of my license plate and levy a fine on me for speeding. I'm glad I didn't invest in that over priced radar detector years ago. One last point: A quote from Benjamin Franklin on the Statue of Liberty reads: "They that can give up essential liberty, to obtain a little safety, deserve neither liberty nor safety." Think about that little statement, my fellow Americans!

***

FEAR

Do you want fear? All an individual has to do to have fear is to buy a newspaper. If you are not fond of reading, turn on the evening news sometime. Most people are not fond of the written word anymore. The 'idiot box' is the place where the media powers that be can assault the senses of the general public, with all kinds of fear-related balderdash. I especially like the Pharmaceutical Company commercials. They espouse the miraculous benefits of wonder drugs; which are being taken, willy-nilly, by unhealthy individuals. Their ad campaigns say: "If you use our magic inhaler just twice a day, you will be able to breathe again!" (Of course see your local drug dealer first: 'The Doctor'). Now, here comes the disclaimer folks, are you ready? Here goes: "Of course our inhaler may have certain side affects. If you experience any bleeding out of your eye sockets or rectum, experience vertigo, epileptic seizures, fungus on your vocal chords, or have the 'shits' for more than seven days, see your Doctor immediately!" They continue: "Some individuals in our test group develop anti-social tendencies, or panic attacks. A few individuals in our control group have experienced sudden death." Now here's the kicker: "85.6% of the people in the group we tested have had their lives improved significantly with the use of our product." (I sure wouldn't want to be part of the other 14.4%.) Now isn't all this helpful information giving you a nice warm, and fuzzy feeling folks? It makes me want to 'hurl' the cholesterol laden fat burgers, I just 'scarfed' up for lunch! I guess all the lawsuits against the Doctors and Pharmaceutical Companies have changed the nature of our TV commercials. It's all really great fun to watch! I love all the banter about evil empires, the economy, and an endless variety of other 'crapola,' puked out at me from the video box every night. We have wars all over the world, famine, pestilence, global warming, dishonest or sexually promiscuous politicians, priests, and teachers. We have drunken, or drugged up Hollywood types, racing up and down Rodeo Drive not wearing panties. We are experiencing higher and higher gas prices, and a plummeting stock market. Add to the mix various local gang bangers murdering innocent children, unemployment, religious fanatics worldwide, who are wantonly killing and maiming people, and the evening news turns into a pretty scary place! I made a decision to not watch TV news programs too much anymore. I'd rather listen to Mozart or Bach, while reading a good book. If I want real excitement, I can paint or write these ramblings from my degenerate mind. It's therapeutic for me! I can always turn on the news tomorrow, if I need a 'fear-fix'. It's just more of the same. Oh! One last thing! Interspersed with all this bad news are commercials about luxury cars, executive type living communities, diamond rings, and inane, cacophonous jingles touting 'happy' fast food establishments. The TV networks always jack up the sound on my TV, for these commercials. Thank God I have a mute button on my remote control! I often think about the poor, working people raising a family, trying to make ends meet, who can't afford a luxury car, much less dining out every night. I wonder what they say to their children? How do they look them in the eye and say: "This is the greatest country in the world?" I pray for these people every night. I pray for myself as well!

***

FINAL THOUGHTS

I am a baby boomer. My generation wanted to change the world. We wanted to make it a better place. We failed miserably at this task. At the same time I pen this diatribe, the inmates are running the insane asylum. My wife Debbie asked me to write a nice book of short stories and here I am on my soapbox once again, spewing vituperative aspersions toward just about everyone, and everything. I am in a quandary! Isn't this what old, retired farts like me are supposed to do in their spare time? I listened to my dad and older brother complaining about the status-quo all the time, before they met the Grim Reaper. Geez! I hope this doesn't mean my time is coming! Oh well, this book is filled with little slices of life, which I have observed, or thought about over the years. Some stories are true, some are fiction. I hope all my stories and reflections make you think and turn off that damned television set for a while! If "they" want you to burn this book someday, hide it in a safe spot!

Sincerely,
Richard J. Cronborg

Retired Heavy Equipment Operator

***

WHAT IS FREEDOM DADDY?

A teenaged girl was having many problems in high school. She was negligent in her studies, homework, and attendance. She hung out with a wealthier group of girls who used drugs and alcohol. The wealthy girls' parents were often not home to provide a family life for their children. Though these children all drove new cars, and had plenty of spending money, they sorely lacked love and parental discipline. The girl in question lived in a humble town home. She had working class parents. She was embarrassed by their station in life. One day she sat at the kitchen table with her dad and asked him: "What is freedom Daddy?"

He got up from his chair, and with his gnarled, calloused hand, grabbed a beer from the fridge, and lit a cigarette. He wore a dirty old bill cap, and gazed off into the distance, thinking for a long while before he began. Finally, he smiled at her, looking into her lovely blue eyes. He started telling a story:

"Once, there was a little black man who was arrested for a horrible crime. He spent many years in prison and suffered all kinds of gruesome physical, and mental agonies. He made a decision after ten years of incarceration, to make the best of a bad situation. He decided to make his life beautiful for himself and others. He learned acceptance. He developed the daily habit of prayer, and cleanliness. He took care of his body, and tried to be of service to his fellow inmates. He learned how to read, and after many years of hard work, became an educated man.

He smiled every morning as he watched the birds in the trees. He valued the panorama of nature, and the changing seasons from his little cell window. The prisoner listened to Chopin, Beethoven, Mozart, Bach, and Handel. He studied music, art, philosophy, and science. In his old age he realized: "They can have my body, but they can't have my mind."

The daughter interrupted impatiently, "Geez Dad, You're not answering my question." "Hold on a second honey," the father said. "We are only half way through." As the Father got a cola for his daughter from the fridge, he lit up another cigarette and continued. "There is another man. He lives in a huge mansion, and owns a profitable business. He drives a brand new Mercedes sedan. He has a lovely wife, and beautiful children. This man is well respected in his business community. He is a proud member of the local, upscale country club. He has more money than he will ever need, and all the material possessions he could ever want. This man is a slave to his job. He worries all the time about the lies he tells his clients, and agonizes over being caught in his nefarious business practices. He cheats his business partner, and his employees out of earnings that they have coming to them. The man has no time for his wife and family when he comes home from work. He resents them, and wishes that he never had gotten married. His wife and children try to avoid him, because he yells at them all the time. His pleasure comes from sitting behind a huge mahogany desk in his home office. He sits in the dark all by himself. He drinks expensive whiskey, and smokes Cuban cigars until he is ready to pass out. He usually stumbles to a leather sofa in his office, and sleeps there in his rumpled business suit, until his children have gone to school and his wife has gone shopping for the day".

The blue collar Dad then looks across the table at his daughter and asks: "Which of the two men is free, honey?"

Without hesitation she replies, "It's the little black guy in jail Dad!" With all that said and done, she jumps up from the table and says: "I'm going up to my room now Pop; I think I might do some homework tonight." She hugs her father tightly for a long time. It seems to him, that it had been an eternity, since she had done that. He looks at her as she bounds up the stairs. He thinks about having another beer, but decides to put on a pot of coffee. He thinks to himself: "They can't have my mind."

***

THE SCHIZOPHRENIC

It began with panic attacks in high school. Actually as he recalled, it began with his feelings of non-being or anomie in grammar school. He lost his composure in church or on playgrounds. His heart pounded, and he knew he was going to die. His was a lonely, solitary, and frightening world. He isolated himself with a bulkhead of books in his tiny bedroom. He lacked rudimentary social skills. He damned his peer group. They tortured him endlessly. They were beneath him.

He experienced further social isolation at the University, but he took honors seminars and became well respected by his academic peers. He finally found his niche. The Professors from a variety of Departments urged him to apply for teaching assistant jobs with them. He turned them all down because he felt he was a sure bet for scholarships at some premier Ivy League Universities.

The breakdown came slowly, like a jungle cat creeping in tall grass, hunting its prey. He felt the perniciousness of it. It was an evil thing which grasped at his psyche with sharp talons. His elegant literacy slowly regressed to an unintelligible string of gobbledygook. He wasn't aware of his psychotic break from reality. He told me they treated him with Thorazine, electric shock therapy, and mood elevating drugs. He added whiskey to the mix. He had therapy sessions with a renowned Freudian Psychiatrist, who put him through Rorschach, and Minnesota Multiphasic personality tests. He wasn't getting better.

He left his parent's middle class home for a seedy one bedroom apartment in the Uptown area on the North side of Chicago. Back in the 60's, Uptown was a nesting place for newly relocated Appalachians from the deep South. They all wanted a shot at the factory, and manufacturing jobs in Chicago.

He became neurasthenic. When he had the energy to leave his room, he sat in hillbilly bars listening to country music, drinking shots, and beers. He spoke to the bar patrons in his educated, stilted vernacular, but was not well received. He was derided and beat up by them. He became the butt-end of their jokes. He stopped washing his body and didn't shave anymore. His parents tried many expensive psychiatric facilities and treatment centers for their son over the years, but he always ended up in some dingy room, in a dangerous neighborhood. He imagined these terrible places as being his comfortable womb. He felt safe in these moldy, furnished rooms…alone.

When he chose to take his medicine, things got better for him. However, he rarely stayed on the medications, and invariably was sucked into a mental darkness. Maybe he felt that he could defeat the dark evil on his terms. At the age of forty-five, he put a bullet in his head. His mother and father found an unfinished manuscript he had been writing. They packed his meager belongings. His suicide made no sense to them. Neither did the gibberish they tried to understand in his notebooks.

***

THE MAJOR TAKES A WIFE

He was a military man all his life. The army made sense to him, because he liked structure, regulation, and regimentation. He retired with a nice pension, a big car, and a nice home. Although he could purchase most anything he wanted, he chose to live pretty much a Spartan life. At the age of sixty-five, he met a dowdy looking female of sixty at a dance sponsored by his local VFW hall.

She had ample breasts, and a nice figure for an older girl. Immediately, he was smitten. She wore electric green, wing type glasses. In the weird frames were the old fashioned, coke-bottle-bottom bifocals, with the etched line in the middle of the lenses. She always wore an ugly hat with a red feather. She had all her teeth, but had spaces between them. She drank vodka martini's and always wore a string of pearls around her neck. She had a bizarre looking shade of red hair under the pill box hat. Lord only knows what her real hair color looked like. After about three martini's her mouth never stopped moving. She prattled on non-stop about the most nonsensical things. They were meaningless things to the Major.

She wouldn't have intercourse with the major until he married her. One their wedding night, she lay stiff as a board in bed. She told him she never really was that interested in sex, only security. He watched her night after night as she put those big old ugly curlers in her hair, and the mask on her face, to prevent her from aging anymore than she already had.

Her whole bed time procedure was frightening for the Major to watch. She spent money like there was no tomorrow. The Major was always frugal, and looked ahead toward the future. He longed for his structured life in the military. How had he come to this? He should have remained a bachelor, since it wasn't such a bad life. Whenever he wanted companionship in the past, he could always rely on the ladies of the night. There were never any complications and he quite enjoyed their company. On, and on, his life went. It was like a slow death. He thought of it as Chinese water torture. He knew he had made the biggest mistake of his life. His was not a problem of structure as he had thought. She wanted him to loosen up, and enjoy life, take a cruise, spend more money on needless vacations, while her snail mouth, and those Venus-fly-trap teeth kept opening and closing. The Major was more lonely than he had ever been in his life. He accepted it as his fate. Nothing could be done, because he was from a generation that stayed married for better or worse. He decided to spend a lot of time on the golf course.

***

OBA

Oba is a poet, who hangs out around the Flat-Iron-Arts-Building in Chicago's Wicker Park neighborhood. This is an area of Chicago where emerging and established artists work and live. Oba washes windows, does odd jobs, and produces mimeographed poetry, which he hawks to people walking by him on Damen and North Avenues. He is there every day, peddling his poetry for pennies. Oba is an African-American gentleman. He grew up in the projects. His face is painted on an old wall of a building in Chicago near the Robert Taylor Homes. The artist did a wonderful job of capturing the dignity of Oba in a beautiful mural. Oba was proud of the mural and always mentioned it to people he'd meet on the streets. Oba got, and deserved his fifteen minutes of fame.

Oba writes about love. His work is simple, but carries good advice and important messages. He seems a happy man. He faces poverty, old age, and illness with great courage. I've never seen this man without a smile on his face, or something nice to say about the day. The artists in the neighborhood love him, and pay him a few bucks for his poems, whenever they see him. Oba buys a pint of wine, or a quart of beer with his earnings. Sometimes he will buy a hot dog or a bag of potato chips. He always has a smile for his customers, whether they purchase his poems or not.

Oba knows much about humility and compassion. His face has lines of character. His eyes still shine brightly. They are a beautiful, hazel-green color. If you meet him, you feel you are in the presence of someone special. He has a special aura about him, only discernable to people who are voyeurs of the human condition. He reminds me of a modern day Shaman. I want to hug him when I meet him and sometimes I do. I feel like I am meeting an important dignitary, in the rags of a hobo, whenever I see him. Somehow I feel he is masquerading; maybe he really is Jesus. He has been a fixture on the corner for as long as I can remember. I own a bunch of his poems. I read them occasionally, and they always make me smile. I was so interested in him, I painted his portrait. He liked it very much. He is one of us. When I show up to hang my paintings in the Flat-Iron-Building, and see him no more, I will know he is with God.

***

THEY ARE SQUEEZING THE JOY OF LIFE OUT OF ME

Politicians, the Clergy, the extreme left, the extreme right, and those in the middle, are squeezing the life out of me. Corporate feudalists, with titanium golf clubs in their chubby little hands, are strangling my humanity. They are all out there like vampires...sucking. My life blood is filling their undeserving, bloated bellies. I am afraid...I am afraid...I am afraid...

Black men, yellow men, brown men, white men, red men...I fear them all on one level or another. I fear women too! Nuns, hookers, feminists, lesbians, and evil suburban wives on the make in the malls, the bars, and the health clubs.

I'm sick of high taxes, newspapers, television, radio, gas prices, video stores, fast food joints, advertising, and endless miles of traffic jams.

I'm sick of AA meetings, rehabilitation hospitals, surgeries, Warfarin, Clonazepam, Vicodin, Advair, Proctafoam, Albuterol, Prevacid, and Viagra.

I fear priapism, high blood pressure, cancer, fatty foods, alcoholic drinks, seductive women, M&M's, and Reese's peanut butter cups.

Thank God I can whack off, and pull boogers out of my nose. I can still wipe my own ass, and go to the public library for free books and movie rentals. Hope springs eternal!

***

FOREVER YOUNG

Guy's in their 60's are driving around in muscle cars right now, playing "Surfer Girl" on their six speaker C.D. players. The dial is turned up to full blast man! It's cause the dude doesn't wear his hearing aids...It just doesn't look cool to be wearing those old hearing aids. Hey man, the dude has his shit together! Can you imagine what his 60-year-old surfer girl would look like in a thong? Arrgh! The picture wouldn't be pretty. I can visualize the dried, saggy, cellulite laden skin, and those icky varicose veins. But hey! 60 is the new 40, don't you know?

Some of the wonders available to my fellow Baby Boomers in this miraculous day and age are: face lifts, liposuction, dermabrasions, lap band surgeries, rhinoplasties, breast implants, penile implants, Viagra, Cialis, pheromones, tanning booths, deep tissue massage, (with or without full release), pedicures, manicures, health clubs, diet programs, ad infinitum...

Somehow, when I see a 70 year old woman in a micro-mini-skirt and five inch stiletto heels, it just doesn't work for me! I am frightened that this dear one might fall, and suffer a hematoma with every shaky step she takes. Yeah, we sure don't like aging gracefully in America. I knew I was getting old when I chose to fart in the gym, and not care who was around to hear or smell the noxious gases leaving my colon. This is a simple joy of old age! We are solid in our maturity, and care not what others might think of us. This action puts an exclamation point on pure, personal freedom!

I don't even want a big, old Harley anymore. I'm afraid my battered legs won't support the weight of the big machine. I am sure my reaction time would cause me to wipe out, and splatter my elderly body on some highway, like road kill. A little Vespa motor scooter seems a more logical choice to me. They get better gas mileage than the big old hogs anyway. I realized this year that no matter how much time I spend in the gym pumping iron, and running on a treadmill, that when I lift my arms up, and hold them out, my old-man-skin is going to hang off of them like chicken fat. This is a major bummer to me. I can't afford plastic surgery. Oh well, I just wont hold my arms out like that in front of any chicks. I'll keep em' tucked in, and flexed! Also, I'll walk around with my stomach sucked in, and my chest puffed out. Hey! I'm still a babe magnet after living on this earth for 59 years, man!

After I strut my stuff in the gym, I go home, check my emails, shower, and eat a killer lunch. Usually I fall asleep in my lazy-boy chair around three-in-the-afternoon. My nicotine gum is still in my mouth, and chokes me sometimes. I'm supposed to pick up my wife from work at the college at five-o'-clock. I freak out when she calls, asking me where the hell I am! Thank God that the college she works at, is only 2 blocks from the house. I say, "Five minutes honey, I fell asleep again." I hear her laughing in the background, as I hang up the phone. Now that I've slept the afternoon away, I'll be up all night watching television. Maybe if I bought that red, V-8 Mustang, convertible muscle car, I wouldn't nap so much! Vrooom! Vrooom!

***

VIDEO STORE DILEMNA

He had just finished his workout at the local health club. It was now a good time to pick up a couple of movies, shower, and relax. Mindlessly frittering away the afternoon, was his game plan.

As he drove home, he pondered which video store was the smartest choice for his movie rental. Hmmm. He could stop at Blockbuster and get 2 movies for around eight bucks, but that was a high-end price. He would be able to counter the inflated price by getting a five dollar, foot-long sandwich, at the Subway Submarine shop across the street. Hmmm.

He continued thinking. The Jewel-Osco food store had the new Red box Videos for a buck. He could rent two movies for two dollars and buy a half-pound of fresh deli meat for four or five bucks, but the Jewel parking lot was a nightmare and so were the checkout lines. Hmmm.

He thought of one more possibility. He could drive to the small video store owned by the Korean, named Hun-Jae. That way, he could get two movies for six bucks. The only problem was Hun-Jae's shop was two miles out of the way, and with gas prices being so high and no sandwich shops in the area, he decided against this option. Hmmm. He felt guilty about not buying from the small business man, but quickly put it out of his mind.

He became so frustrated by these mental machinations that he gave up and decided to drive straight home, watch some crap 'B' grade movie on cable TV and ferret around in his pantry for a can of chili. As he ate the chili, and stale saltine crackers he discovered in the cupboard, he was angered by his thoughts of the New America. He remembered the good old days, when telephones had rotary dials, and all a man had for entertainment on TV was three channels. If the rabbit eared antennae couldn't pull in a clear picture, he could always take a walk in the park, look at the beautiful sky and smell the fresh flowers. These were less complicated times, he thought. For him, in this new world, even relaxation had become too complicated.

***

SAME PLACE, SAME TIME

He was retired now. It was an early retirement for him at fifty-five. His body just couldn't do the hard physical labor anymore. The doctors told him that he would die if he kept on working. He received a small pension and a disability check every month. He woke up with his wife every morning at the same time. He drove her to work in his beat up truck. She was happy as a lark to be driven to work and picked up at night, when her days' work was done.

When he got back home in the morning, he sat in his lazy boy chair smoking cigarettes, drinking black coffee, and reading his newspaper. At 11:00 A.M. every day, he gingerly climbed the stairs to take a shower. He left the house every day at 11:45 and always arrived at his local tavern by noon. You could set your watch by it.

He sat on the same raggedy bar stool, in the same dark corner of his chosen watering hole, every single day. Dawn, the bartender, greeted him with smiles and warm hello's, as she poured him a double scotch on the rocks, with a water on the side. The bar opened at ten-in-the-morning, but he always arrived at noon. He knew that only alcoholics drank in the morning. He and the other customers watched the news on TV and shook their heads in anger and despair. Suddenly, the mood changed, and all of them laughed and joked about some quirky human interest story. At one o'clock, the TV set was changed to either soap operas, vile audience participation shows, or baseball. At 3:00 P.M. every day, the man left a generous tip for Dawn, and headed home for his nap. He always had three-double-scotches at the bar...no more, no less. When he got home, he set his alarm clock and took an hour nap. When he woke up, he brushed his teeth vigorously and rinsed with mouth wash. Then, he picked up his sweet wife. He did this every day at 5:00 P.M., except on Saturday and Sunday. He helped her prepare dinner and washed the dishes, while she read or did cross word puzzles. He poured himself two cocktails every night after dinner...No more, no less. He massaged his wife's aching shoulders or feet, between puffs on his cigarette.

At ten-o'-clock each evening, the man and his wife kissed, and went to their separate bedrooms. This routine went on for five years until one morning, the man died in his lazy-boy chair. That evening his wife called and called for him to come and get her. Finally she had one of her co-workers bring her home. She had a bad feeling in the pit of her stomach. She found him with a newspaper in his lap, a cold cup of coffee, and a pack of cigarettes on his end table. The TV was still on.

***

THE DINNER DATE

They were beautiful people, single and available. Both were in their mid-30's. He was a successful stockbroker. She practiced criminal law. He made reservations at a chic Bistro in an upscale part of the city. They both had attended the right schools, and dutifully had graduated with the highest honors. Both were impeccably attired for their first meeting. They had manicures, pedicures, and facial treatments. He had a hundred dollar haircut. She had a perfectly coiffed hair-do. He wore an Armani suit. She wore a Vera Wang original.

They had all the bling and swing, man! They were power people, on a power date. It was a meeting of upscale hipsters who talked the talk and walked the walk. They met and smiled at one another showing their perfectly capped, whiter than white teeth. All went according to Hoyle. The introductions were perfectly rehearsed. They had done their routine on dates a million times before. They both knew the ropes in regard to their presentation of themselves. The wine list was magnificent, and the young gentleman knew how to order. They tittered and fussed over how wonderful everything was in the restaurant. He made sure she observed his Oyster Rolex, and she brushed her hair from the diamond earrings which graced her comely earlobes. Neither was a good listener. They were too self-absorbed. They parted with joyous exclamations about how successful their first date had been.

As he stepped into his Mercedes sedan, he mumbled to himself, 'pretentious bitch'! She wasn't much happier about the time spent with him. As she entered her Porsche convertible, she muttered to herself, 'another misogynistic asshole'! She started her sports car and angrily slammed through the gears, as she sped unsafely, back to her gated community complex.

They both got back to their respective domiciles at approximately the same time. They went to bed and masturbated...He had his orgasm, while watching a porno flick. She used her vibrator as she thought of some old college flame who 'rang her bell', back in her old sorority days. Amazingly, they both reached orgasm at the same time! Ah, the joys of autoeroticism!

***

THE DISHWASHER

It was a fucking hot summer', he thought. At least I'm on the day shift in this joint" He was a 25 year old dishwasher, with a drinking problem. He worked in a huge, upscale restaurant-cocktail lounge, next to a motel, near the city airport. He arrived at work every morning at 6:30 A.M. He always hid a pint of Old Grand Dad in his small carry all bag. He parked his beat up car in the parking lot, in back, by the hotel. The restaurant owner told him not to park in front of his place because the car looked like shit. "Fuck him", the dishwasher thought, but he complied with the owner's demands anyway. He went to his locker, hid his stash, and took his street clothes off. He put on his 'whites'. They were starchy-assed, funky-looking, and stiff as hell. He hated the fucking things...The pants were always too short or too long, and the fly had fucking buttons, which would come undone at inappropriate times...The waitresses used to laugh at him and make lewd jokes about his pecker hanging out. What added insult to injury was the little fucking white cap they made him wear. "I look like a fucking ice-cream man", he thought to himself. He punched the time clock before seven and leered at the waitresses. Some of them were doing "tricks" at the motel in back of the restaurant, when their shifts were done. The girls had to make ends meet any way they could, when the tips weren't too damned good. He knew this for a fact. He saw the 'John's' taking them in and out the doors...

He liked to embarrass them by waving and yelling at them. He liked Rosie, the Italian woman with the big tits. She still looked really good for a woman in her late 40's. He also like the red-head named Terri. She wore those sexy, push up bras that forced those beautiful globes of her flesh, out of the top of her uniform. Last but not least was Angie. She was a little bleached blonde with the tightest ass, and shortest skirts he had ever seen in his life.

"What a great fucking job!", he thought. "They bring me bus pans of dirty dishes, and I get to have a hard-on all day long!" They paraded in and out of the hot kitchen. It was busy as hell in the restaurant from seven-thirty till ten a.m. He slammed trays of dishes into the steam washer. The conveyor moved the clean dishes out to the back, where some old, 'wet-brained,' retard put them away. The dishwasher yelled and screamed at him, when the old dimwit couldn't keep up, or broke them because they were wet, or too hot to handle. The dishwasher hated the forks that poked him under his fingernails. He got infections from the slimy shit that went under his fingernails. He also had a bad case of acne from wiping sweat from his face with his dirty hands, and the steam constantly pouring out of the machine. He was quick at wiping the slop from the plates, and stacking them into the trays. He slobbered the uneaten food into a hole in the stainless steel countertop and the mess fell into a gray industrial-sized garbage can underneath the counter.

He smoked cigarettes while he worked, but couldn't piss or shit till 10:30 a.m., when things slowed down. Then he would go to his locker, get the pint of whiskey, and guzzle half of it down. Then he proceeded to that shit-hole of a bathroom to wash the filth from his face and hands and take a long piss, and a good dump. Sometimes he put on a new starchy white suit, if he had too much garbage on his chest, or if he was soaking wet. Before the lunch hour rush, he had to check on deliveries of fruits and vegetables, potatoes, and boxes of frozen meat. He peeled rotting potatoes, because they used these for hash browns. He vowed never to order hash browns ever again!

He liked it when he took the service elevator down to set up the conference rooms for meetings and luncheons. It was dark and cool down there. He usually helped a waitress do the set-ups. Some of the waitresses showed him a little leg or tit, or talked 'sexy talk' with him, while he was doing the set-ups. Sometimes he produced a twenty from his tattered wallet, and got a blow job. When he was broke, and the waitress-whores aroused him too much, he had to go in the shit-hole bathroom and whack off, before the luncheon dishes started coming. Luncheons really fatigued him. He usually caught up around 2:30 or 3:00 p.m., then everything had to be wiped down and sanitized for the next shift, and the dinner rush. He liked leaving everything spotless for the night crew. When all was in order, he brought what was left inside the whiskey bottle into the bathroom, locked the door, and chugged it down. He then undressed, and dumped the filthy 'whites' into the dirty clothes receptacle. He washed himself up real good, punched out, and then asked one of the cooks what was good to eat on the menu that day.

The cooks were good to him, and loaded his plate with meat, potatoes, and vegetables. Management allowed him to have ice cream, pie, rice pudding, anything he wanted to eat at the end of his work day. This was the only meal he ate all day, so he ate a lot. He needed his money for the tavern, his cigarettes, gas, and the rent for his furnished room. He worked nine hours a day, six days a week, with Mondays off. Usually, he went to the racetrack, or to a ballgame on his day off. He had an uncomplicated life, and everyone at the restaurant liked him. He thought, "I have it made!"

***

THE ARTIST

He was lucky enough to have a modicum of success in the art world. He lived in New York, near Chelsea. The arts district was a stone's throw from his roach-infested tenement, but the light was good in his studio, and sometimes he slept in better digs, due to the mercy of wealthy females who 'just adored' his work. He lacked health and dental insurance, and had to go to the free clinics when he was in pain. This happened more regularly now, as he approached his mid-fifties.

He was an early riser, and had brushes in hand by eight-in-the-morning. He usually drank free wine and finger foods at art openings during the week, to defray the cost of his grocery bill. He liked to drink single malt scotch when he was on a roll selling expensive paintings; but now the good times were few and far between. His youthful good looks had left him bankrupt, and he was no longer the golden boy of the art world. In the place of his full head of long, jet black hair, muscular lithe body, and full beard, was a balding gray pate, a scraggly goatee, a whiskey nose, and a considerable paunch. His glory days were over, but he felt he was painting the best work of his life. The gallery owners mostly ignored him now, so he had to live by his wits. This consisted of finding sugar-mommies and sugar-daddies to purchase and promote his paintings.

He usually worked on a painting 5 or 6 hours a day, then his 'muse' would leave him. In its' place came the scotch bottle.

He sipped, and listened to Miles Davis, Chico Hamilton, or down-home, Mississippi blues music. He got drunk and scanned the day's painting with his artist's eyes. He saw where the painting needed to go, and what he needed to do with it to make it beautiful. He felt the glow from the booze in his belly, and generated an ideational process for the next days' work. Sometimes a thought of genius would strike him right between the eyes, and he would begin working once again. He smoked reefer and cigarettes, and drank scotch till the wee hours of the morning, until he could see no more. Than he would pass out, exhausted, into his bed.

He loved the life. For him, it was all about the art. He still wore expensive clothes to his art openings, to keep up appearances; but the collars of the fine shirts were fraying, and the expensive shoes he wore had holes in the soles. He stuck cardboard inside of them, so his feet wouldn't get sore or wet. He reasoned that he had to frequent upscale-type watering holes in the city, to continue to develop relationships with wealthy new clients. He never was sorry that he had denied himself a corporate life; with a good, solid retirement annuity, or medical and dental insurance. The only thing he really regretted was that the youth and verve had left his body. He was an educated man, whose mind was peaking. His creative juices were in their prime. He pondered philosophical questions many an afternoon with a drink in his hand. He watched the cigarette smoke curl up toward the ceiling, as Coltrane blew his horn. Grandiosity grew in him as he drank. He knew that his 'big break' was just around the corner. He looked forward to drinking with his old art buddies in the evenings. It was a ribald, drunken fraternity of braggadocio and self-absorption.

These are our unheralded heroes: Poets, writers, actors, models, singers, artists, musicians, and photographers. There are millions of them all over the world. They all believe in their hearts, that they are going to be famous someday. After all, that 'big break' is right around the corner.

***

WHY CATS HAVE IT MADE

Somewhere it is written: "Soldiers love dogs, while artists love cats." I suppose a person has to have a somewhat feminine side, or an artistic-creative nature to love cats. I just can't picture a John Wayne kinda' guy with a big leather leash, and a spiked collar attached to the pencil neck of some 'puddy-tat'. That type of weird scenario just ain't happening for me!

I had the good fortune to own two feral cats, or perhaps they owned me. My wife found them when they were little kittens, living under our deck, outside of the sliding glass door of our family room. She started cooing at them, offering them bologna and cheese. They came crying at the screen door every night. My hard, black heart began to melt. Before I knew it, we adopted them. We were paying for cat litter boxes, shots, checkups at the local veterinarian's office, cat toys, scratching posts, balls, fuzzy toys, catnip, litter, canned food, and cat treats.

My God! It was like having another baby! These lovely little animals were always aloof, disobedient, noisy, and hairy, but Lordy they were cute! All they did was eat, sleep, play, look stupid, and chase 'non-existent-entities' that I didn't see. They were nice in the winter, when they chose to curl up in my lap while I watched TV. They eventually started peeing and shitting wherever they pleased. My wife informed me that they were afflicted with some type of 'cat-neurosis'. Yeah sure, I wanted to wring their fucking necks! I dealt with their mental problems, in the manner any blue-collar guy would. I threw em' in their travel boxes, and donated them to the local animal shelter. It was one of the toughest things I ever had to do in my life. I think we had them for 4 or 5 years. For me, dumping them there was like putting my child in a place that had a gas chamber. Because of my guilt, I haven't been able to enjoy a bologna and cheese sandwich for a long, long time. My wife says I did the right thing, since we couldn't allow them to be peeing, and spraying all over the new carpeting and the walls. We had just paid a contractor to remodel a number of rooms in our home.

Today, there isn't hair all over the furniture or on the floors. My emphysema has improved. The incessant crying, and the ability of the felines to get under my feet in the morning when I groped to make my coffee, is but a distant memory. In spite of it all, I have to admit, I still miss them. They provided me with calm, comfort, undying affection, and a joy in watching them execute their role in God's Great Universe.

My wife still misses them terribly. I know enough not to bring back to her memory the joyful days when we each had a cat in our lap. Women have long memories of their husband's misdeeds. I don't want to open any more wounds. I tread lightly now, after 29 years of marriage. I should have been born a cat. Man, would I have it made!

***

ODE TO JOHN

John the jokester, the boisterous Irishman, always took it to the edge. He knew more jokes and stories than anyone I had ever met in my life. Just when I thought his antics would get us tossed out of a bar, he'd back off, and sing a song of love and humor to the crowd. He possessed this uncanny ability to know just how far he could go with his foolishness. Everyone loved him. Then the asshole in him would come out again. He was fueled by Irish Whiskey. He was on a mission to destroy himself with it. Laughing all the way to death, and desolation, he had a subtle knack to bring anyone he touched along for the ride. Everyone loved him anyway. He greeted the sun in the morning with a shot and a beer, wearing a smile on his loony face. Phoning me early, my wife answering, he told her he was going to make me a rich man someday. He even had her laughing at his blarney. Sometimes, even she was tempted to believe him. All he wanted was a drinking buddy at eight-in-the-morning. That was my friend John. You would love him, if you ever had the opportunity of meeting him.

He ran a bulldozer on a job with me. I cleaned up his mistakes. The boss knew I was covering for him. "The guy should be fired," the boss would say, but he liked John too much, to put the hammer down on him. You had to love him. When he was drunk, which was all the time, he let me drive him in his Cadillac convertible, to empty quarters from condom machines, in men's rooms. We hit many of the bars, all over the north-side of Chicago. We threw bags of quarters in the trunk of the car, 'flying' from bar to bar, like honeybees traveling from flower to flower. We never, ever, had to buy a drink. If the ladies didn't know and love John, they knew and loved him before we left the bars. He was handsome and had an uncanny, magnetic, drunken charm. Onwards, onwards, he always went, a million-miles-an-hour. He was flying with the eagles, in this, his 'hey day'.

Things got worse for him because of it. I couldn't carry him anymore. The caddy got smashed, then the beater pick-up truck. His drinking made him unemployable. He lost his driver's license. He lost his union card. He lost his girlfriends. He lost his city connections. Finally, he lost his freedom. I lost touch with him. I asked around for a long time. Nobody knew where the hell he was. What had become of him? He was lost to me, but I still loved him.

Finally, I was giving an hour of my time to orange clad prisoners at Sheridan Medium Security Prison, in Sheridan, Illinois. I told them my life story. I tried to tell them how I turned my life around, and how I managed to stay clean and sober. Applause came to me after my talk. A man came up to me, blind in one eye, which was clouded over. He had an ugly, deep knife wound across his face. He was fat, and looked ill. This person, was John. He hugged me and told me he was serving 3 years. He had a year to go, and he would be free once again. Too many DUI's and nefarious activities had put him in the 'slammer'. He told me he was gonna' rise up again, just like the Phoenix. He knew all the right strings to pull. Caddies and dames and big jobs were going to be had by him once again. You had to love him.

***

GORDON WISCONSIN

It's way up there man! Somewhere around Hayward. Fifty-miles from Telemark, where they hold the famous cross-country ski race known as the Birkenbeiner. My friend Jake sold his tool rental business, and bought a big house with a tavern in the basement. He had twelve cabins for campers, and rented snowmobiles, bass boats, and fishing gear. He also sold worms and beers. He owned a pontoon boat, a Piper Cub equipped with struts, and pontoon landing devices which allowed him to fly clients to all the lakes in the area, on up into Canada. He lived on the Chain-of-Lakes, and the view from his living room in the main house was breathtaking, and spectacular. In the morning, we drank 100-proof-Wild-Turkey-whiskey, chased by Leinenkugel beers in the bottle. We'd go outside on the porch, and shoot red squirrels with our .22's. Jake said they were nasty little creatures, and needed eradication. I don't remember why, but was happy to help him with the task. We chopped firewood in our t-shirts, listening to the jack-pines crackling from expansion or contraction. It was a dry ten degrees, and I was sweating from the effort! It was sure nice to be 25 years old, by God! We went to the local tavern and ate bacon and eggs, with coffee. Then we bought a loaf of bread and some hot dogs, before heading out to God only knows where, to hunt snow shoe rabbit. Around noon, we'd start a fire, roast the hot dogs, and have a couple of beers. We'd come back home and watch an eagle fish in the lake. Its talons extended, and with a "whoosh" in the water, the glorious bird accelerated into the sky with its' wiggling prize.

The fire in the main house was warm, and me and Jake reclined in two big lazy-boy chairs, wiggling our toes next to the fire, our woolen socks still on our feet. Jake was a man's man. He was built like an ox. He knew how to operate and fix machines. He could drive just about anything. He was 35 years old, ten years older than me. We played a lot of poker together, raced motorcycles, and went fishing and hunting. We were always in trouble with our wives. The town of Gordon had a three lane bowling alley, way back in the mid-seventies. An Indian lad was the pinsetter. I liked Gordon, Wisconsin. I'd hate to think it has changed, but my logic tells me otherwise. Jake couldn't make a go of the resort. I tried to find him for a long time. He was a helluva guy. Maybe someday, our paths will cross again.

***

I'M A BADASS TECHNO PLAYA'

I got me an ipod, a blue-tooth, a Wi-Fi, and a Hi-Fi. I'm so bad, I'm connected and wireless! I got me a flat screen TV with four clickers man! There's no frustration with mega-pixilation. I got surround sound, and mega bass, if you ain't diggin' it, I'll get in your face. I'm on My-Space, and You-Tube. I'm clickin' my mouse to stay in the groove. Ebay and Google, I try to stay frugal. Save on gas, and you will be last! Mustang Cobra makes me smile! Ten miles to the gallon, gotta' maintain my style!

Gotta' keep upgradin' cause I'm on the fast track, but my credit card limits are breakin' my back! It aint my fault, dog! I'm speakin' true! The faults with the corporates, they're tryin' to screw you. I like a job, if I can get up late. The clubbin' scene is what is jake. I'm underpaid cause it's a conspiracy. I blew off high school, but hey! I'm getting' my GED.

I'm goin' to Hollywood to make it big! I got dreams man, cant you dig? Manual labor ain't for me, I'm a badass playa', cant you see?

***

PYRO

Pyro, formerly known as Stanley Liebowitz, originated in upstate New York. He lived in a lovely home, with successful, educated parents. At 18 years of age, he started doing menial jobs. His parents were crestfallen. They wanted their son to be a doctor, attorney, or a stockbroker. At 19, he rode off on his Harley-Davidson Road King. He gave them the finger, as he left home and never returned.

Pyro headed for Sturgis, South Dakota, the Mecca for outlaw bikers. He settled outside of town, and did odd jobs to survive. He kept to himself, and pumped iron in his cheap room in a boarding house. He grew massive arms, and a broad chest. He shaved his head, and had an ace of spades with wings tattooed to the middle of his forehead. He was one scary looking dude. He bought leather vests, chaps, and bags for his Harley. When he drank in local bars, he became sullen. People didn't mess with Pyro. If they did, he kicked their ass. Usually he just wanted to drink, smoke a little weed and be left alone. One day when he was drunk and bored, he set fire to an old barn. Pyro never experienced anything like it before. The rush he got, was better than sex for him. He felt a strange power. He felt better than he did after sex with a good-looking hooker. He was smart, and careful about his newly found love. He studied different types of incendiary devices, and became quite facile at getting away with the arsons. He set over one-hundred fires in five years, without getting caught.

Finally, the law of averages caught up with poor Pyro. He was apprehended by the local police. Lives had been lost. Stanley is doing life without parole at a maximum security prison. The prison guards light his cigarettes for him, in a fire-proof room, during his exercise time. He is not allowed to smoke anywhere else. They say his eyes still light up, when he sees the flame from the Zippo lighter.

***

THE HERO

He was a tall, gangly kid, with blazing red hair. He stood a head above his peers in grade school. He wasn't very athletic, and denied the opportunities presented to him by coaches, to play basketball.

He was the object of derision, and laughter. He had a learning disability. What was even worse, he stuttered. He suffered through the embarrassments with a valiant stoicism. The kids were mean to him, but he seldom struck out at them. He merely bottled it up inside, and found comfort in the drink later in his life. He lived in a humble suburban home with his mom and dad. He never had luck with women and remained single. He is in his mid-40's now, still not married. He gave up the booze to take care of his elderly parents. His brothers and sisters abandoned them, but not "Red". He owns his own one-man, carpentry business. He has huge hands, and swings a hammer with the best of them. Red always has work, because he believes in quality at a fair price. He does pretty damned well for himself. One day, on the way home from work, he saw a man in a car, drowning in a pond. It was winter-time, and it was freezing. Without hesitation or fear of personal endangerment, Red jumped in the lake and broke the window of the car with his claw hammer. He gave the man CPR and mouth to mouth, just like he had learned in the boy scouts. He covered the old man with painting tarps from his pick-up truck, and called 911 on his cell phone for the ambulance. He held that old man in his big arms till the EMT's arrived on the scene. Red didn't realize he was shaking like a leaf, till they wrapped him up and put him into the ambulance alongside the old man. He had saved the old man's life.

Red never told anyone about his heroics. Newspapers, radio, and TV stations bothered him for a while. I found out about his act of heroism from someone else. One time at a coffee shop, he told me he was just a wifeless, lonely workingman. I told him he was the most important guy I had ever known in my life.

***

ON WOMEN

I love women. I always have. They are supernatural. They are too glorious for this earth, this vale of tears. I didn't notice them until 5th or 6th grade. I was too busy groveling in the dirt, playing marbles with other dirty little boys. We had patches on the knees of our blue jeans. These little girls blind-sided me. It was like taking an unexpected right cross to the jaw in the tenth round! There they sat in all their glory, in those sky-blue, Catholic school girl uniforms. They were fresh, beautiful, and clean. They were little Madonna's with hands clasped firmly in front of them on their desks. Their knees were clasped tightly together, to keep us from seeing their hidden treasure. Their mothers taught them properly. They were guarding that holiest of holy possessions, the doorway to future progeny, the vagina. I looked at the girls. I wanted to smell their hair. I wanted to kiss their lips, and touch their smooth cheeks with my dirty little boy hands. They were a cut above the boys, and they knew it!

We were the dogs, or snakes and snails, with puppy dog tails. The girls were smarter than we were. A few of us were as smart as the girls. We usually derided these unlucky boys. In seventh and eight grades these girls started to develop breasts. These creatures were sought after, and highly prized by us. We began to clean up, comb our hair, and wear our father's Old Spice Cologne.

In high school we thought we were smarter than the girls. We were wrong. We tried to score with the easy ones and treated our steady girlfriends like queens. We learned we were never good enough for them. They were right! We whored around, drank alcohol, when some old wino would buy it for us, and smoked cigarettes. We thought the true measure of a man was what he wore, what he drove, how much money he had, and how good he was with his fists. Our girlfriends knew better. They continued to be smarter than us! They appreciated a boy who wrote poems or love letters. They loved a boy who would dance with them, and send flowers. They wanted a boy who was headed for college and showed them good manners. We didn't get it! These boys were pansies to the guys in my neighborhood.

Luckily, I went to college. I finally tasted their red, ruby lips. I got to smell their hair. I stroked many a fair cheek. I adored the nape of a woman's neck. I cupped and sucked those breasts...the Holy vessels which held the milk for mankind. I touched their soft white thighs, and kissed their warm ears and necks. My hand wandered to the warm, secret place between their thighs. I was at the heart of the Universe! What we were doing was mystical and important. As I entered these wonderful women, we celebrated a most important primal ritual. We rejoiced in orgasm!

As I aged I came to realize that lovemaking had to have a morality to it, if it was to be of any value. I finally understood the commitment of marriage. I finally realized why these little girls held their knees tightly together, in grammar school. They knew then what took me twenty years to learn. I told you they were smarter than us!

I failed at my first marriage. I tried again. My second marriage is heaven on earth! I am a lucky man. I still gaze in wonderment when I look at my wife. I wonder why she stayed with me through all my bad behavior. We have been together for almost 29 years. I appreciate her so much more now, since I have matured. My daughter is twenty-five years old. She is lovely, just like her mother. They both amaze me! I know they are smarter than me. A man can never be as important as a woman. Carrying a baby, and giving birth to it, is by far the greatest thing a human being can do. Loving your baby and caring for it, brings a parent close to God. I'm glad I can participate in the loving of my child. I am also grateful that my wife and I are still in love. As I age, I am still in awe of women, but in a different way. When I see beautiful young women now, I no longer lust for them. Instead, I want to father them. I want to give them fatherly love and good advice, if they ask me for it. Helping mankind gives me purpose and makes me smarter.

***

ON MEN

I never trusted men. They turn on you. I always preferred the company of women. As a kid, I was a punching bag for other boys. I don't think the anger left me, until I was in my fifties. I learned how to box, wrestle, play football, and baseball. I learned how to run bulldozers, cranes, work drill rigs, pump iron, run marathons, and drink large amounts of whiskey. I did all the "man" type things which are valued by men. It's all a brutish and boring game. I'm sorry I wasted so much time with it.

Men began to accept me, and look up to me, when I was in high school. I learned how to be violent. I learned how to fit into a man's world. The number of real man friends I have, I can count on the fingers of one hand. I'm starting to learn that real men are the one's who love to help the weak. I'm leaving my male posturing, in favor of little random acts of kindness. For me today, that is what my "maleness" is all about. The rest of it is solid bullshit.

***

LAP DANCE

A quiet desperation brings them here.
The sun is high...hot and humid outside.
The lounge door swings open...It's cool inside.
It smells of perfume and disinfectant.
Hip new sounds are coming from the juke box.
The young women sit, or stand.
Mixing with the male customers...they ply their trade.
The men sit, and drink. They smoke cigarettes.
They laugh...Some sit still, and sullen.
Some are young...Some are old...
All are here for the same reason, cheap thrills.
Safe, impersonal, self-gratification.
Have the girl of your dreams for five minutes.
You pick her out,...Ten bucks,...and a five dollar tip,...
Only if she makes your dick good and hard.
Drink that booze, and loosen up...
Feed a few bucks in the juke box.
Wait for your lovemaking songs...
Pretend she is yours...
But remember, do not touch.
"She really likes me," becomes their mantra.
Two or three lap dances with this special one...
No cops to worry about.
Never can get a phone number...
Maybe this time.

Leave the bar eighty bucks lighter...
Go home and masturbate...
Thinking of her face, tits, and fine ass...
For as long as you can...remember them.
Masturbate until it all fades into oblivion...
Then back to the bar...for another lap dance.

***

AMMO

They called her Ammo. Her real name was Ann-Marie. She was blonde, and buxom, a full-figured lass. Heavy mascara, lipstick on her face like a mask. A miniskirt adorned her well-proportioned ass. She sat sweating on the floor, of a bedroom, in a basement. Although she was no whore, men were waiting for her to service them for free. The blow-job was her specialty. She enjoyed the camaraderie. She took all comers, while on her knees. It didn't matter to her, it was her joy to please. The music blared outside the room...soul music of the times...the chosen tunes. The booze flowed freely, the party raged on. No one would stop it...It was like dropping a bomb on her humanity. I wasn't in line, it wasn't for me. I still was guilty, don't you see? That was the key. How could we allow such crimes and not see? We reveled in the tragedy of poor Ann-Marie.

***

THE FACTORY WORKER

He entered the same door every morning and went to his locker. He was a big man, five feet ten inches tall, weighing around three hundred pounds. He wore a gray, industrial colored shirt, and gray pants. His belly hung over his belt. He had a crew-cut and didn't smile very much. He carried a black metal lunch box. He wore steel-toed shoes and thick white socks to cushion his swollen feet.

He promptly punched in at seven a.m., every morning. He always made sure to punch in five or six minutes early. He was 28 years old, and had been working at the factory for ten years. He started there immediately after his high school graduation. The company liked his work. He had perfect attendance. He never missed a day. He took a half-an-hour lunch break in the lunchroom, every day at noon. He punched out at three-thirty. He bought a six pack of beer on the way home, and every evening sat in front of his TV set, eating and drinking. He lived alone in a cheap apartment not far from the factory. He didn't like to socialize with people too much, and didn't have much to say. He rarely smiled. At work he was all business.

He operated a huge punch press. His was set up to shear steel. He stood at his station on a rubber mat and fed plates of steel in the monster machine. He measured and scribed the cuts he made on the steel with a soapstone. He wore hearing protection to save his ears, but lately he noticed a ringing. He loved his job, and was proud when the foreman came by, smiled at him, and patted him on the back.

One day, he was distracted by something. He pushed the sheet of steel in the press and the huge cutter blade sheared off eight of his fingers, clean as a whistle. He gazed at his mangled hands for what seemed like an eternity. He passed out, and when he woke up his hands were bandaged up, like huge boxing gloves. No one from the plant came to visit him in the hospital. No flowers were sent. The doctors managed to re-attach four of his fingers; but he was told his hands would never be the same.

After recovering for a month or two, he got off worker's compensation. He was glad to get back to work at his punch press. Everyone was glad to see him back at work. He wanted to stay at the factory for 47 years, until he could collect his social security, but times were hard, and they laid him off after forty years. He couldn't find another job. He was damaged goods,... lousy mangled hands,...plus, he wasn't qualified for anything, and was too old,...they told him. He did odd jobs, sweeping, cleaning, night watchman, pizza delivery man, but he missed the old plant. One night after picking up his six pack and eating in front of his television set, he died of a massive heart attack. A few of his tavern buddies came to the funeral. No one from the plant signed the book at the Funeral Home.

***

THE BOXER

At the age of ten, his snaggle-toothed, alcoholic father, saw him getting the shit knocked out of him by two older boys, in the gang way of their apartment building. The old man threw open the ramshackle window of their kitchen and barked: "If you don't kick their ass, I'll give you worse when you come back inside!" The ten-year-old stood his ground, and fearlessly took them both on. He came out of the altercation, victorious. He was scared of the old man. "Not bad kid," the drunken old sot mumbled to himself. He tended to the boy's wounds, and gave him a buck to buy some ice cream. The little boy smiled, and hugged his dad. Rarely did the old man show the kid any kind of affection.

Another little boy lived down the street. His father hung him by his hands with rope, on beams in the basement of their apartment building. He whipped him with a leather belt across the back, when he wasn't obedient. The boy had lash scars across his back. The two fathers drank together, and one day in the tavern, they decided to buy their boys boxing gloves, build a makeshift ring, and teach them the 'manly art of self defense'. These two fathers epitomized the lowest type of sadistic behavior. They drank, and watched their sons box, until the boys were bloodied like a couple of pit bulls. If one of the boys started crying or whining, he received verbal abuse from his father. They were made to continue in the lunacy for a whole summer. Strangely, after a few months, the boys began to enjoy the sport. They shared a special bond.

As the boys grew older, they grew apart. The boy who was abused, ended up beating his father within an inch of his life. He left home after that, and joined the Marines. He lost his life in a fire fight in some dense jungle in Southeast Asia, Viet-Nam in 1969. The other boy was in trouble all the time in high school. A coach put him in the ring, and he won a Golden Gloves Championship competition, in Chicago. He decided to fight professionally, after having a stellar amateur career. Academics were never his forte, so he did what he knew he could do best. He fought for a long time. He never got the money he deserved. He couldn't read well enough to understand the contracts. All his managers, trainers, cut men, promoters, and attorneys, stole his money from him.

He fought his last fight at a place called DaVinchi Manor, in the Austin neighborhood, on the west-side of Chicago. He was a worn-out 40 year old. He had cuts over his eyes, and people threw garbage at him. He was laughed at and scorned. He was a has-been. He was lucky enough to get a full time job in the Chicago Laborer's Union. After about ten years of laboring, he began to notice the tremors in his hands. He visited a doctor, and found out that he had Parkinson's disease. The doctor told him he had taken too many 'shots' to the head. He had double vision sometimes, and started getting a cataract on his left eye. He had cirrhosis of the liver, and was told by his doctor to cut out his drinking. Finally, he applied for disability insurance from the government. Luckily, they gave it to him. It was a pittance, but he made good with it.

Towards the end of his life, on Sundays he visited the grave of his friend, who he was forced to box with as a little boy. In his prayers he used to say, "Sleep tight my friend"; "You were a great warrior." "We will be together again someday soon." "You know you were my best friend in life." He then would go to his furnished room, and make home made soup. He let it simmer a long time, just the way his mother had done years before. He filled the tub with hot water, and soaked the arthritis out of his bones. He enjoyed these Sundays. He watched sports on TV, and ate the soup while sitting in his old chair. He thought to himself, "I gave my best all the time in this life". He was proud of that fact. He knew it was his trust in God's will, that would sustain him till the end. He died alone, a veritable pauper at the young age of 55.

***

WHAT THE HELL CAN I EAT?

Yesterday, I read in the newspaper that I couldn't eat my precious red tomatoes anymore! Horrors! There is a Salmonella outbreak once again in America. This means I can't eat pizza, or have them put tomatoes on my tuna sandwich at Subway. I purchase my tuna sub every Friday, on my way home from the gym. Now they tell me I can't eat the jalapeno peppers, which I have Pablo put on the Submarine sandwich as well! What the hell can I eat?

My doctor has me on rat poison, (Warfarin) for my peripheral artery disease, which means I can't eat anything containing vitamin K. This edict disallows me from enjoying spinach, lettuce, and all green leafy vegetables. I used to eat these to stay healthy. Vitamin K is also in all the protein drinks I used to enjoy to build my muscles, so I could look like my heroes: Hulk Hogan, Arnold Schwarzenegger, and Sylvester Stallone. The Vitamin K is also in my power-protein bars. These bars are nasty tasting blocks of muscle building components, although they look like candy bars. They taste more like dog biscuits, but they do the job to assuage my desire for sweets.

I can't eat my beloved Krispy Cremes or Snickers bars, because I'm a high glucose kinda' guy. I sure don't want type-2 diabetes. I've been reading that we don't get enough vitamin D, but cheese and ice cream raise my cholesterol, and I fear a heart attack. I'm also told that 20 minutes a day in the sun will give me plenty of the 'D', but I fear skin cancer. I spent most of my life in the sun, as a heavy equipment operator, and I look like an elderly version of the Sunshine raisin claymation characters on TV. I am told I shouldn't eat too much red meat. There is too much fat in that stuff. Yet, my doctor has me taking iron supplements, because I am anemic. I don't get this reasoning at all, since red meat supposedly has sufficient iron in it to keep my blood healthy. Hmmm. I guess I better stay away from the red meat anyway, because the cow ranchers can't afford to feed their cattle decent food. The cows are so weak and sick that before they are butchered, they are laying down on the ground, dying.

I fear McDonald's, Wendy's, Taco Bell, Arby's, Barone's Pizza, Dairy Queen, and Colonel Sander's Kentucky Fried Chicken. I am told a glass of wine or two every day is good for the heart and circulation, but I am a recovering alcoholic so I can't take advantage of this particular joy. I sure don't want to end up in a alcohol treatment facility again! I can't eat fish, because of the PCB's, and mercury poisoning. My wonderful dark licorice is a 'no-no' because it is said to interfere with my blood thinners, and raise my blood pressure. I long for the old days. People smoked, drank, laughed and lived their lives without any fear. The old timers never thought about dying, ate whatever the hell they wanted, and some of them actually lived to a ripe old age.

I think I'm gonna' go to the ball park today. While I'm there, I'm gonna eat three Chicago style hot-dogs, slathered with mustard, relish, onions, and tomatoes. I will eat the white bun, and love its' empty calories. The sesame seeds can have their way with my beat up colon, I don't care! I'm gonna' drink a couple of sugary lemonade's, and eat a couple of ice cream sandwiches. I'm gonna' sit in the bleachers, get sunburned like a lobster, and have a helluva time cheering on my Chicago White Sox! I made a decision to be happy today! When I get home from the ball park, I'm gonna' hug my wife and watch mindless TV shows, while I jam Cheetos, Snickers Bars and licorice in my 'pie-hole'. Damn! Ain't life grand!

***

TAKE A LOOK AT THINGS

Yes...take a look at things.
Take a look at things, from a new perspective.
Turn pictures upside down, gaze at them, and find new worlds of thought.
Ask yourself, How long it has been since I went alone someplace beautiful, to watch a sunrise or a sunset? Take a look at things...
Nothing ever shows its true qualities with a quick glance.
Take the time to really see what you are looking at.
Let your mind's eye define the shapes, colors, and textures it encounters.
A whole new way of looking at reality, is yours for the taking if...
You really take a look at things.
Slow down, breathe slowly, and deeply.
Unfetter your mind, dismiss all thought, and take a look at things.
Emptying the mind on a daily basis takes practice, but reaps great rewards.
Don't think. Sit as still as you can in the silence.
Exist in the Now, then take a look at things.
Don't judge what you see. Don't label what you see.
Just let things be...in their true essence.
Take a look at things...Look at the wonder of all natural things.

See trees, flowers, animals, rain, snow.
Leave all man made things alone for twenty minutes a day.
If you take a look at things in this way...
Your world is going to change dramatically...
Your mind and body will begin to heal.
You will have your own secret place to go every day.
You will find peace...
So, take a look at things.

***

THE CORPORATION MAN

He knew he had a black heart. The company machine sustained him. A drip bag containing a steady supply of money was jabbed into his vein. His black heart pumped with power, fueled by the plasma of ill-gotten gains. All the gears were in place, each one synchronized to move him in specific ways. He knew the corporate dance. He was a marionette on strings. He was a corporate man through and through. He was always one step ahead of the game. He lived by his wits and never rolled snake-eyes, because for him, there always was a plan B. He was as snaky and swarthy as he had to be. He was after all, a corporation man.

Many a battle he had won. He was tried and true...He was number one. Then came the breakdown of the great machine. What to do now? Corporations made times lean. No more people to buy the stuff. The cost of gas had made it rough. Mortgage plans ran askew. What the hell was he to do?

First went his mansion, then his cars, his stock in utilities, airlines, and bars. The 401-K went into the shitter...His wife left him for Paris, all in a titter. They finally did it to themselves as well. It doesn't bother me, I'll make out well. I got me a guitar and a bottle of booze. Dylan said, "When yah ain't got nuthin, yah got nuthin to lose."

So I expect to see revolution again. Civilizations have their cycles and this is the end...of the America I knew. Democracy

isn't for only the few. So hear me corporate feudalists that be...
Load up your guns...gotta' watch out for me!

***

JUMPIN' JACK FLASH IS A......HUH?

You knew it was coming! Gas prices in America are skyrocketing. Heeee! It's a gas, gas, gas, man! Really it's not a very funny thing, dudes and dudettes. The tree-huggers don't want us to drill up in Alaska. Yet, they continue to live in 15,000 sq. ft. homes and fly around all over the place in their Lear jets, to save "humanity". What bullshit! It makes me want to cry after watching another Oprah show, or the View...Arrrgh! The Democrats say we need to tax the windfall profits made by the huge oil companies. How are these companies going to finance the drilling projects? Of course Exon-Mobile made near a twelve billion dollar profit the last quarter of this year. Hmmm. Maybe the Democrats are right. Tax the profits, and the gas companies just raise prices...It is a definite no brainer who gets hurt in this deal. Tax, tax, tax, and who the hell pays for it all. You know the answer...Hard working, honest, middle class people. Thank God the Senate has enough Republicans in it, to stop needless spending. But, the Republicans are just as bad. A lot of buck-passing is going on in that community of evil-doers. The rich keep getting richer and the middle class of honest, hard-working men and women pay the lions share of tax dollars. Yeppers, folks, that's my story and I'm sticking to it. Whew! Everyone I talk to is confused. What is the truth? It's India's fault, it's China's fault, it's the fault of the OPEC nations. Who the hell is responsible for all of this? I don't really know...But here is my solution.

We need a national strike. All you hard working blue collar guys, waitresses, office workers, store clerks, auto mechanics, middle management guys, and gas station attendants need to take a month off. Yes! It's a party month man! Buy a lot of booze, and potato chips...stock up on hamburgers and hot dogs. Rent a bunch of cheap dollar movies, that you can mail back to the video store. The only rule is don't shop, work or drive for a month! Heeee! Is this an evil plan? Make love, have BBQ's, love-ins, meet your neighbors you haven't seen for a million years. Find out who lives on your block. Swim in each others plastic pools and work on your tans! This is old fashioned 60's style revolution for the hell of it! God bless you Abbie Hoffman! Watch corporate America just freak out! It's gonna' be great fun! I bet you, within the time frame of just one month, a lot of prices are going to come down, and come down dramatically! We will affect the whole global world market, man! We will show our power! The power is held in the calloused hands of the middle class, if we choose to take it! You, through your well thought out American activism, will help re-established the values once upheld by our forefathers who planned the Boston Tea Party. NO TAXATION WITHOUT REPRESENTATION! Put that in your pipe and smoke it you shameless politicos. You Democrats and Republicans should hang your heads in shame. You have failed us miserably! It's time for the middle class, to kick some major ass! Corporate America will finally get what it deserves. We live in an Oligarchy now, not a Democratic government. A solidarity of black, white, yellow, brown, and red workers are going to rise up against the machine. They've pitted us against each other long enough. We know who the real enemy is now. Better lock your gated communities nice and tight! Remember workers, you have freedom of speech, freedom of choice. You have the right to bear arms against any enemy of the Democratic way of life. It's guaranteed to you by our great Constitution. Congress recently tried to take this right away from you! What a travesty of justice! This is a God-given right for all free men and women in a Democratic society. Don't let anyone tell you any different. They are blowing smoke up your ass, and cluttering your minds with bullshit. Now let's get busy, and organize! One last thought...You people on the dole, who generationally let the government coddle you, and give you welfare money for nothing...get off your bar stools, and find a job! AMEN.

***

THE PIZZA DELIVERY MAN

Back in the mid-seventies he got a buck for every delivery he made, plus tips. He was smart enough to work Friday and Saturday nights. These were the money nights. He did this job, after punching out at his factory job. Monday through Friday, usually forty hours a week, he worked at a chemical plant. During his day off on Saturday, before his pizza shift, he cut his grass, shoveled snow, or worked on his cars. He paid his bills, replaced sump pumps or garbage disposals. Sometimes he painted walls, or hung that lousy wall paper that his wife wanted in the babies' room. He hated hanging freakin' wall paper. Sunday was set aside for church, and brunch with the family. The mid-afternoons were owned by him. He fell into his lazy boy chair to drink beer, and forget about his life of drudgery. He watched sports on the TV.

On Fridays he carried a gym bag with clean clothes, so he could shower the filth off his body from the factory, and put on the clean 'stuff' for the pizza delivery job. He spent the two hour interim between jobs, in the local tavern drinking beer. When he opened the door of the pizza joint, he immediately was hit by the heat, ringing phones, and people running around behind the counter. The guy who owned the place smiled broadly at him as he walked through the door. The owner was dressed in whites. He made pizzas, and watched them carefully, as they simmered, in the big Blodgett oven with the revolving shelves. The owner was proud of his oven and the secret recipe for his pies. He made a pretty damned good pizza. Years ago, he worked as a milkman and, along with his wife, raised four boys. He saved his money and bought the shop when there was nothing out there but cornfields. He knew in a few years that the cities' urban outcrop would envelop his shop, and that finally, he would have it made. It happened just the way his visualized it. He became involved in local community politics to secure his business and his family. Now, he drove a big Cadillac. He earned it through sweat, and foresight.

The delivery man did pretty well for himself. He made forty or more stops a night. With tips, he usually made around seventy bucks. He also took home a free pizza at the end of his shift. In those days he only spent five bucks for gas, for a whole night of driving around. He started delivering at 5:30 p.m. and left the shop by 1:00 a.m. The job was grueling. The driver had a big aluminum, insulated pizza oven sitting next to him in a bucket seat. It was too big to stick in the back, because he drove a compact car. He was only cooled by the breeze from open windows in the summer months, because his work car had no air-conditioning. He hated deliveries to apartment complexes, because he had to roll up all the windows, and lock the car; otherwise thieves would get into his pizza box. When he got back into the car, he would have to roll all the windows down. The sweat rolled down his forehead, and got into his eyes, until the temperature inside of the car came down. The delivery man's key to success was taking five minutes to route his deliveries intelligently. The owner loved how speedy his 'guy' was, and bragged to all who would listen about what a good worker he had. The delivery man knew all the streets, and was quick and efficient. He ran hard and fast, up and down the stairs. He was young and knew this was keeping him in shape. Sometimes lonely old hags would open the door, showing him their played-out tits. Their apartments stunk of cigarette smoke and booze. Their breath was putrid from smoke, whiskey, and periodontal disease. The old broads tried to entice him into sexual encounters by saying, "Come back later baby after your shift is done." "We will have cocktails. I'll be here waiting for you." They winked at him, or licked their red lips lasciviously while looking at him. He smiled at them and said nothing. They rarely tipped him. Lonely homosexual men tried to make dates with him. They seemed frightened by their advances to him. He guessed that they feared getting a black eye.

The delivery man liked the solitude of the night. He was his own boss. He changed the radio station in his car, at will. He sang his songs and dreamed his dreams. He watched the people enjoying their Friday and Saturday nights off. He slowed down when he saw good looking women on the street. A couple of times, he was beat up, and robbed of his money. The owner always had him call the police, and make out a report. The owner never asked him to pay the money back, which was stolen from him. After every delivery run, the pizza shop owner had his drivers cash in, so they didn't carry a lot of money.

Winter time was tough. The driver wore thick wool socks and combat boots. Delivery times were slowed by ice and snow on the streets. The side streets were the worst. He sometimes had to run a half-a-block with the pizzas, because of parking problems. By the end of the night, his feet were wet and frozen. He was glad to have the hot pizza oven in his car in the winter. He warmed his frozen finger tips by placing his hand on top of the oven, as he drove his route.

His wife constantly complained about being left home alone on the weekends. She also complained about wanting a better house, and a brand new car. She shopped for expensive clothes every evening, while he was working the pizza job. She was a beautiful young woman…the kind that turned heads. She had long black hair, a pretty face, and a beautiful body. She had a set of legs that were 'custom made' for high heels. He loved her deeply, and tried to provide all the good things she demanded. After a year, he blew off the pizza job. He bought that big dream house in the suburbs, and new car for his wife. He knew he couldn't afford them. After another year, their marriage ended in disaster. He saw what a lazy bitch his wife was, and how she had used him. He went back to his old boss at the pizza shop to beg for his delivery job once again. He had to do something to pay child support now.

***

THE PHOTOGRAPHER

She was an inquisitive little kid. She was a chubby little girl, with blonde hair and freckles on her nose. 'Tomboy', was a perfect description for this ball of energy. She played Cowboys and Indians, or Army with the boys in the neighborhood. Playing with the girls was just too boring for her. She hated phony tea parties and dolls. Her mother was heartbroken. She wanted a girlie-girl. "What's the matter with you honey?", her mom used to say, "Don't you want to dress in up in pretty dresses"?...The response for her daughter was always, "Naw ma', I like blue jeans and flannel shirts." She liked the comfort of them, and she didn't have to worry about getting dirty.

Her father laughed in amusement. He had great times with her! They watched baseball games, and shot basket together in the grammar school parking lot.

Her life changed when her dad bought her one of those cheap, drugstore Brownie cameras. She took pictures of everything. In a couple of years, and after about five or six camera purchases, she advanced to a state-of-the-art, mechanical, 35-millimeter Nikon camera, with all kinds of different lens attachments. Her dad helped her build a darkroom, according to her specifications, and she was on her way to fame and fortune.

She won all kinds of awards for her photography in high school and in 1964, she received a full scholarship to Stanford

University, to continue her wonderful obsession in the Fine Arts Department. In 1968, the Viet Nam war was raging hot. At about the same time, she received her Fine Arts Degree. She hired on with a National Photo Magazine and begged them to dispatch her to Viet Nam. She saw it as her duty to be a photo-journalist. She marched 'point', with grunt Marines in some of the most devastating fire fights. At first the military wouldn't let her go on these dangerous missions, but she ingratiated herself with some powerful military men, and ended up getting her way. This was her nature. She was forceful, but always with good intent. She wasn't the type of individual to be denied.

She was the bravest of the brave. They nicknamed her, 'little bit'. She was so much more than that. A lot of times she tucked her precious camera away to tend to the wounded men, administering morphine, packing wounds, clamping severed arteries, and all the while saying prayers. She was known to pick up an M-16 from a dead Marine, and help hold off the enemy. The men loved her. 'Little Bit' became a legend among these rugged men. She sent heart wrenching photos, and stories back to the Magazine. All in all, with a few R and R's, she spent more than three years in Viet Nam. She came home changed forever.

She suffered through Post-Traumatic-Stress-Disorder, and malaria. She lost a few toes to jungle rot. In her later years, she suffered from exposure to Agent Orange, a devastating chemical which was sprayed all over the jungles. She survived a double Mastectomy, and beat colon cancer.

Today, at the age of sixty-two, she is happily married to the same guy. They just celebrated their 28th wedding anniversary. He is a professor of Art History at a University here in Chicago. She has three grown sons, and eight grandchildren. Only one of the grandchildren is a girl. She favors this one. She is always in trouble for teaching her how to throw a baseball and shoot baskets. She has a bad 'ticker' now, but she doesn't let it slow her down. She says, "If I buy it on the basketball court, it would be a great way to go!" She plants a beautiful garden every year and enjoys taking pictures of wildlife and flowers. I once told her she was an extraordinary woman. She looked me straight in the eye and told me, "You're full of it!" She said, "Sometimes I don't know where you find room, for all that nonsense running around in your head!" Talk about special, she is one of a kind.

***

EATING CONTESTS AND OTHER BIZARRE EVENTS

A person can generally gauge the decline of a society by its' citizens interests. Ancient Rome is a good example of this truism. Political treachery, debauchery, and last but not least, the mauling of gladiators and slaves in the Coliseum, proliferated in ancient Rome before its decline. A once great and noble Rome, fell eventually because of a pernicious disintegration of its' moral fiber.

Fast forward, if you will, to America...This is the America we all know and love today. The year is 2008. One totally bizarre spectacle, which astounds me is the eating contest. It baffles me how a young girl, in her early 20's, can stuff 100 hot dogs down her gullet in ten minutes. She only weighs one-hundred pounds for goodness sakes! This is an amazing feat of gluttony! The supporters of this so called sport call it an Olympic event. People who are really good at it can earn upwards of a hundred thousand bucks a year! People flock to see these well advertised abominations, and what's worse, these events are televised. Gluttony, (one of the seven deadly sins), is on National TV! Way cool! The next thing we are going to see are drunken Circus geeks eating live chickens. Naw, that wouldn't fly. More likely, the American viewing audience would prefer live crucifixions. We could really get off on a good old fashioned crucifixion. Now we're talking turkey!

***

VIOLENT AND IMMORAL TV SHOWS

Also on television , we have guys in screened, octagonal rings, just beating the hell out of each other. They can kick, punch, and bite, (if the referee looks the other way). They wear light weight boxing gloves, and most of the competitors have cauliflower ears. These men are mean! The visual array of tattoos, worn by most of the fighters, looks quite menacing.

We have video games which celebrate criminals blowing cops away. Many of these games also champion graphic pornography. Don't worry, because children under 18 can't purchase them. What do yah' think your twelve-year-old brother is going to be doing in your bedroom, when you are out on a date, trying to screw your girlfriend in your muscle car? That's right! He's gonna' be messin' with your game. He's gonna' be getting' off on that neato sex and violence stuff!

Modern day wrestling is no better. The 'so-called' sport, is a lewd carnival of juiced- up behemoths, both male and female. Female wrestlers have the silicon bags to make them more comely. Somehow the giant quadriceps, and beard growth, cancels out the erotic pleasures produced for the audience from their "fun-bags". Men cut their foreheads with razor blades, to fake the aftershocks of phony head butts. All in all, it's a pretty disgusting scene. What really blows my mind, is that a good percentage of the fans think that what they are witnessing is REAL!

Then we have the butchy looking females, participating on roller derby teams. They really frighten me! Ouch! I can tune in any night of the week, and watch drug and alcohol rehabilitation patients, weeping and whining about their wasted lives. I can view women who have snapped, and murdered their families. I can enjoy rapes, murders, pornography, horror, autopsies, a vast cornucopia of stuff which afflicts my good mental health and general well-being. This is prime time America!

Mainly, I feel sorry for the kids. I wish I could bring them back to the times when we watched prime-time Walt Disney features. I wish they could watch Leave it to Beaver, the Dick Van Dyke show, and Dobie Gillis. What happened to good, wholesome, family entertainment in this country? It isn't strange now to see Mom go to one room for her TV shows, Dad goes to another room for his shows, and the kiddies go Lord knows where. I just hope that the parental controls on the television set and the computer, are set where they ought to be. I seriously doubt it.

***

MY BEST HIGH SCHOOL TEACHER, MR. RACKY

He taught at an Augustinian Catholic High School for boys, on the South side of Chicago. A diminutive little man, standing all of 5 feet, 5 inches, weighing a mere, 120 pounds soaking wet, he was a giant of a man to me. He wasn't a bad looking man. He had black and gray, salt and pepper hair, cut in a crew. He dressed well. He always wore crisp white shirts and a narrow conservative tie, which was very fashionable at the time. He rolled up his sleeves, and showed his veiny, nicely muscled arms. He always demanded our attention and respect while we were in his classroom.

I was a junior at the time. The year was 1965. I heard rumors about how tough his class was for academic honors students. I was one of them. We all were college bound. Every kid I talked to told me I was going to hate him and his class. They were all wrong.

I decided to listen to him and write down everything he said in his lectures. I learned about prose, verse, poetry, and great literature. Mr. Racky was fervent about it all, because he loved teaching. He was totally dedicated to his chosen profession. He expected all his students, through his tutelage, to metamorphose into fine readers and writers. He expected excellence from each and every one of us. He was always available in his office after school hours to go over any fine points that we did not understand. He, in essence, offered his life and his knowledge to us. He believed in, and loved all the literature which he required us to read.

We discovered the world through reading, Upton Sinclair, Jack London, Ernest Hemingway, Fyodor Dostoyevsky, Camus, Cervantes, E.E. Cummins, Walt Whitman, Henry Miller, George Orwell, Ray Bradbury, James Joyce, Herman Melville and Ralph Ellison, to name a few.

Mr. Racky prepared me for what I was to encounter at the University. At college, a student was expected to write endless themes and papers. Essay tests were the norm in the days I was a college student. Mr. Racky taught me how to write a good paper. He taught me how to organize my thoughts and to be a good rhetoritician.

This man could have made much more money teaching in the public school system, but his heart was at St. Rita High School. He passed away a few years ago. I received the news in my alumni newspaper. I like to think that Mr. Racky would have been proud of me. I went on to receive my liberal arts degree. I'm sorry he is not here to read the books I have published. He probably would have shown me all my typographical errors and misspellings! It is amazing what an impact a single, solitary man can have on so many, in a life that is directed, and dedicated to the good.

***

HUMILITY

I wouldn't know humility if I tripped over it. I desire it, because it is worth pursuing. The humble individual is at peace with himself and with God. It takes a great deal of practice and self-reflection for a person to engender in himself any measure of humility.

I think the less I think about my selfish needs, while taking action in doing little things for other people, the more I understand humility. We live in an ego-oriented society. People become unhappy when the can't acquire wealth or status. I'm learning to give up my ego. It isn't easy. I fail miserably every day, but I keep trying to be a better listener. I try to be of service to people who I meet in my everyday life. I try to give a smile, and a pat on the shoulder, to the unhappy ones I meet. I need to open doors, and carry bags of groceries for the elderly or infirm. I never thought of these things when I was a young man. I realize that in death, we all must give up our egos. None of us are more important than anyone else. We all have equal value in the great universal plan.

I am at peace, and more humble, when I have quiet times. I do this through prayer and meditation. I empty my mind of all its transient thoughts, and exist in the now. All is right in my life when I do this simple practice. I get a special, peaceful result every morning when I meditate. I liken it to taking my boat out on a peaceful lake, early in the morning,...alone with nature. Me, the worm on the hook, and sweet mother nature.

Five or ten minutes pass, and I get to 'play God' with the fish. I catch, then release, the beautiful fish back into the water, to live another day.

Let your friends and enemies off the hook, dear readers. Always forgive their human errors and misunderstandings in regard to you. Forgive them, because it does you the most good. Say you are sorry, even if you know you are right. Give up your anger, because it is poison to you and your fellow man.

These are lofty ideals for sure...but they are worth nurturing in yourself. I keep failing at them, but more importantly, I keep trying.

***

THE CALL GIRL

She lived in a nice neighborhood. Hers was a squeaky clean kind of life. She grew up in a typical upper-middle class suburb. She was bored at a very early age. She was a very intelligent young girl, with a high I.Q. She hated grammar school because the girls made fun of her frizzy hair. Her mom and dad loved her, and provided her with ballet and music lessons. She liked doing the girlie things, like playing with dolls. She was a girl scout, a choir member, and went to church with her family every Sunday. She was never sexually abused in any way, and had a normal childhood. She started high school, and developed many friendships with boys, rather than girls. She always liked men more, because she had a voracious sexual appetite. She felt women were petty and hypocritical, in regard to their sexuality. From the age of twelve, all she ever thought about was sex. She possessed a gorgeous body and face, and lost her virginity at the age of thirteen. She was very selective in regard to who she went out with in high school, but boys, being boys, rumors traveled quickly, and she was labeled with the reputation of a whore.

In college, she realized she had no use for small minded people. She studied finance and business management. She decide to start her own business. She began to have sex for money her freshman year. Usually it was with older men, who valued her quality of being discreet. She also liked the idea of sex with married men, because she always held an ace-in-the hole, if they decided to cross her. None of these men would much appreciate their wives finding out about their dark secrets.

She amassed a considerable amount of money in college. She went out on an average of 2 to 3 dates a week, enjoyed the sex, and banked enough money to purchase a nice condominium in the heart of the big city, where all the action was. She received a business degree, and graduated from college with honors. Her parents were proud of her. She lived and maintained a double life. It was easy for her. She had her rules, and stuck by them. Hers was a business of one. She didn't trust any other girls, and didn't want any men involved. She only had 'dates' with wealthy gentlemen. In time, she had a black book with names of some very wealthy, and influential men. She was totally trustworthy. Confidentiality was the keystone of her business. She also took wonderful care of herself. She dressed and conversed like a society woman. She loved her life, and reaped many rewards from her chosen profession. She could smell a phony a mile away. She was practical, and had good common sense. She made her first million dollars by the age of thirty. She made contributions to charities, and had many friends both male and female. She became a silent partner in a variety of businesses, to explain the source of her income. Her wealthy clients were more than happy to cover her tracks for her, in order to present her as an honest business woman. Everyone, other than her clients, thought she was a high-powered business woman. No one ever suspected otherwise. She never wanted a husband or children. She loved culture and variety in her life. She went to art galleries, and the symphony. She amassed a valuable art and book collection, and enjoyed fine dining. She kept her secrets into her old age, and luckily lived a life without any complications.

She realized how fortunate she was, because the odds were against her to pull all of this off. It all could have gone horribly wrong at any moment. She was always a woman who knew what she wanted, took the risks, and ended up doing very well for herself. She died comfortably, surrounded by her dear friends, with a smile on her face.

At her wake, her female friends were amazed at how many fine looking elderly gents were in attendance, and the vast array of flowers she received from them. Baskets, wreaths, easels, and sprays for the casket filled the whole viewing room of the Funeral Home. The Funeral Director had tears in his eyes. He had been one of her most loyal customers. At the cemetery, a wealthy male traveling companion gave her Eulogy. Somewhere in his speech he said, "She will be missed". These words were a 'whopper' of an understatement!

***

BOB...VIET-NAM VETERAN

He was a neighborhood guy. I didn't hang out with him. He went to public high school. He smoked cigarettes and cruised the streets at night. He was a tough fellow. He never picked on me, and I appreciated him for that. He went to Viet-Nam for a year. He was in the Army. He is 61 years old now. He did time in a Federal prison, for selling explosives to the wrong guy. He lost his beer truck driving job. This was a tough thing for him to lose. When he was released from prison, he lived with, and took care of, his elderly Mom and Dad.

When his mom died, his brother got power of attorney from Bob's confused father. In essence, his brother screwed Bob out of his legal inheritance. I recently helped Bob retain an attorney, because he beat up a guy who was tailgating him. His mom and dad were in the back seat of the car. I know some high powered attorneys and was glad I could help my old friend. Bob has been out of work for quite some time now. He calls me up sometimes and we go out for pizza and talk about the old South-Side of Chicago. Bob has diabetes, and needs surgery on an enlarged salivary gland on the left side of his face. He still smokes and drinks beer. He threw his insulin away because one of his doctors at Hines Hospital got him 'pissed off'.

Bob met me at the gym today. I told him, "For Chrissakes' Bob, you gotta' get back on the insulin and watch your diet!" He said, "Yeah, yeah, yeah,...screw it!" "I eat a dozen eggs every morning, a pound of bacon, drink, smoke and enjoy life!"

"What the hell!" Recently, he told me of pain in his feet and numbing and tingling in his legs. I told him to get his ass over to Hines hospital (where they treat veterans of foreign wars in Chicago). I told him, that his symptoms sound like diabetic neuropathy to me.

I told him I would do a computer search, and print out any salient information he might need about the disease. Bob was really thankful. I did the search, and print out for him this morning. I really like Bob. He's been beat up pretty much by life, but he is a survivor. My south-side Chicago buddies seem to be going down fast now. I've been going to quite a few wakes, lately. I gotta' make sure I'm a stand-up guy with my old Chicago buddies. They seem to mean a lot more to me now. I look forward to having pizza with Bob on Thursday night.

***

JUST ONE

I don't want just one,
I like to fly...
One is too many.
A thousand aint enough.
I like to fly, you see,
Like a big assed bird in the sky.
Why drink, and not get high?
So I must deny, just one.
I'm a son of a gun, when I'm on the run.
I drink huge quantities.
I'm an upscale bum.
Ain't no difference between...
A pig in a slum, or a limousine.
A pig, is still a pig.
An alky, is still an alky.
An addict, is still an addict.
I tried again, and again...
To drink with pleasure.
I thought I merely needed...
To measure.
So, I drank just one.
I blacked out, and woke up with the scum.
A conundrum to be sure...

I saved my life, I took the cure.
I took it...
Just one day at a time.

***

WALMART

Oh great monolith, I adore you for your cheap underwear! Of course, the Chinese dye irritates my skin. I forgive you for the empty store fronts in our small American towns. You great, bullshit, monolith...You are the one, who put Mom and Pop out of business. We are so proud of your low prices, which are subsidized by American taxpayers. We love your shitty products and anti-union sentiments. Health benefits and wages for your employees are minimal. They have to go on Medicaid and live in Section-8 housing, to make ends meet. The American taxpayer has to pick up the tab, because of you. Your employees shop at your store. They owe their souls to you and the Walmart way of life. Your employees are treated like modern day sharecroppers. I love your commercials on TV. Bend over and smile, faithful employees. Something wicked is coming your way. Walmart is a family store. The pervasive company philosophy is to "do more with less". Of course, the employee has to work more, and he or she, is paid less. Your employees have to work 'off the clock' to survive. Is Walmart an evil company, my fellow Americans? If you think so, shop at the mom and pop stores, even if you have to pay more. If you do, you are saving our American way of life.

***

THE GAME HAS CHANGED

I liked it when a man's handshake was his bond.
No contract has to be signed. No attorneys had to be present.
The game has changed.
I liked it when men settled their differences with their fists...
Then, they shook hands after the battle.
No guns or knives were ever used.
Both men got to walk away with their dignity, and their lives.
The game has changed.
I liked it when companies were loyal to their employees.
Men did an honest day's work, for an honest day's pay.
The game has changed.
I liked it when young people gave up their seats on a bus...
Or opened doors for little old ladies.
The game has changed.
I liked it when the future looked bright for me and my family...
The game has changed.
Soon, I will be dust...There still will be sunshine and blue moons...
People will laugh and cry...

Babies will be born, new wars will be fought...
For me, the game will be over.

***

BILL

I went to grammar school with Bill. He was a tall, blonde, good-looking kid with a great smile. He had a pleasant, easy-going nature. We went on campouts together, when we were in the boy scouts. He ice skated better than anybody in the neighborhood. He was fast and nimble on the ice. Bill was poetry in motion. He loved to play hockey, and when the sun went down and everyone went home, there he stayed on the ice, smiling and gliding under the light of the full moon.

He was a gentle soul. Everybody liked him. He didn't laugh at me, even though I stumbled on the ice in my brother's skates, which were two sizes too big for me. I had to wear 3 pairs of wool socks to make them work. The other kids laughed at, or ignored me, but Bill took me by the hand, and put his arm around my shoulder to share the 'magic of the glide'. He knew the ice was a special place. It was pristine, clear, and beautiful. He wanted me to experience his joy. I appreciated his kindness.

Forty-five years have passed, since those idyllic days. Don't ask me how. It all went by too fast. Yes, a lot of time passed, before I got a chance to see my dear friend again. Oddly enough his house was located only 20 minutes away, from mine. One of my other friends from grammar school, named Russ, prepared me for the reunion and for what I was about to see.

We drove into a nice neighborhood. Amidst the fine homes, and manicured lawns stood Bill's house. Once it had been beautiful, but now was hopelessly disheveled in just about every possible way. The roof needed repair. The grass, weeds and trees were overgrown, looking like a mess. Old cars, tools, and garbage were in the driveway and garage. Bill motioned to us from a basement window to come around to the back door.

I entered and stared death in the face. Bill looked to be around 70 years old, even though he was only 59. The dank smoke from his cigarettes hung in the air. The basement was filthy dirty. Garbage was strewn about everywhere. I observed old newspapers, lumber, and ashtrays overflowing with cigarette butts. I hugged Bill and smiled. My friend Russ told me, that Bill had decided to drink himself to death. He had been drinking and smoking excessively for three years. He was a five-pack-a-day man now. He also managed to drink 30 cans of beer every day. He rarely ate much of anything. Bill had been falling down a lot lately. He carved a staff for himself, from some deadfall in his backyard. He looked like an alcoholic Moses.

The living room of the house was as filthy as the basement. Bill still had a wife. I didn't meet her, but I met his two sons. They were strong looking young men, and reminded me of what Bill used to look like as a teenager. The boys wore bill caps, and were smoking cigarettes, just like their dad. Russ told me that I would want to leave Bill's house after being there for five minutes. He was right. I couldn't breathe in that place. I grabbed one of Bill's arms and helped him up the stairs. We were taking him to dinner at some local, dive tavern that Bill liked to frequent. Bill's eyes were vacant. He didn't remember too much of the past. I don't think he knew who I was at first, but I jostled his memory.

I told him about the ice, and how good he was on it. I saw the cloud lift from his face, and the twinkle return to his eyes.

It was just for a few seconds, like the sun peeping through the clouds, only to be covered in darkness, once again. He picked at his food in the bar, and left most of it behind. He continued to drink cold steins of beer we ordered for him. I told him that I brought him a present. It was my Memoir...The first book I had published. I told him it had tales of the old neighborhood, where we came from in Chicago. I wrote a nice letter to him inside the book jacket, and signed it for him. I hugged him, and kissed him on the forehead. We both had tears in our eyes. I picked up the book for him, when we left the bar. He had forgotten it. We drove him home and I promised to visit him again soon. Russ and I both waved goodbye to Bill, as he sat sadly, in the basement window. In Russ's car I looked at him and said, "Gee Russ, he really looks bad, man." "He looks like an old man." Russ said to me, "I told you so." "He sleeps a lot now, and when he isn't sleeping, all he does is smoke cigarettes and drink beer."

Russ and I had lunch in the neighborhood near Bill's house today. For some reason, neither one of us mentioned his name. We should have gone to visit him. He was only ten minutes away. As I was driving home in my nice sedan, I knew I had to write his story. I promised myself that I would visit Bill tomorrow. I only hope that tomorrow isn't too late.

I never went back to his house. After a week, my conscience began to bother me. I called a couple of times and left messages on his answering machine. Bill never returned my calls. I think he just wants to be left alone now.

***

ENVY

I never understood why some individuals were envious of the accomplishments of other people. Maybe they lacked the ability to take action in their own lives. I try not to waste my time pondering the psychological dynamics of these individuals, but lately circumstances have caused me to keep thinking about them.

These people anger me. They are dream stealers. Their joy comes from belittling the accomplishments of people with good intentions. I think their envy, and resentment toward the doers, comes from their own low self-esteem. These grouches are glum, structured people, with shallow mental dimensionality. They are afraid to color outside of the lines, or think outside of the box. Most of them are lazy. Many of them are procrastinators. Most of them are losers.

The best way to deal with the jealous ones is to laugh. When they belittle what you have accomplished, or make light of your efforts, just tell them to have a nice day. Better yet, tell them that you will pray for them. This really pisses them off! I enjoy this form of sadism. It's good for my mental health. When my friends paint a beautiful picture, or get a brand new car, I like to celebrate their success. I'm happy when someone I know, gets a promotion at work, or writes a new novel. These are the people I want for my friends. They are people of action who forge ahead, believing in themselves. When others around them say they are going to fail, they work harder to assure themselves success. I'm proud of people who display these traits.

Even if they fail, they learn invaluable lessons. Thomas Edison's teachers thought he was a dullard in his youth. Mr. Edison failed countless numbers of times. He said later in his life that each failure brought him closer to success. Edison was right. People who don't do anything, never make any mistakes. They just flounder in mediocrity. Believe me when I tell you, practice makes perfect. Have the guts to follow your dreams. Always dream big. You'll know you are a success when the "green-eyed-monsters" around you make light of your accomplishments.

Someone once asked Albert Einstein, "What is the most important quality that a human being can possess?" Without a moment of hesitation, the great man answered the interviewer's question with one word: "IMAGINATION"!!!

I still don't know what I want to be, when I grow up. I do know one thing. I'm busier than I have ever been in my life. My life is full of joy because I do things! I don't have time for envy. I can't control what the grouches think of me. I'm too happy and free, because my hard work and imagination liberate me!

***

THE BICYCLE MECHANIC

The guy was a natural mechanic. He lived down the block from me, on 72nd and Spaulding Avenue, on the South-side of Chicago. It was the late 1950's. I must have been around nine or ten years old. On hot summer days, I went to his open garage to watch him work on bikes. His whole garage was filled with chains, wheels, bike frames, inner tubes, tools and all kinds of paraphernalia, useful in the art of fixing bicycles.

His name was Myles. He was a big guy, with a dark sun tan. He had a huge beer belly, and big greasy hands. I never saw him without a smile on his face. He worked in his garden in the morning, but sought the shade of the garage, and ice cold beer from his fridge, every sunny afternoon. It was there, where he would build his bikes. He was retired, and having the time of his life. The radio was tuned to the afternoon baseball game, or those old 1940's tunes. He and his wife danced to them at the Willowbrook Ballroom, after the Second World War. If she saw me standing out there, she brought me lemonade and cookies. She would say, "Here you are honey, I see you are here to help Myles again." I would say, "Yes, ma'am, thank you for the lemonade and cookies."

I didn't own my own bike. I wanted one more than anything in the world. My mom and dad didn't have the money to buy me one. Myles liked me a lot. I didn't say too much, but watched everything he did with his tools. He taught me how to re-pack wheel bearings with grease, patch inner tubes, true bent wheel rims, straighten out spokes, and put chains together. Although I didn't realize it at the time, I was learning how to be a bicycle mechanic. The kids in the neighborhood laughed at me all the time, because I didn't have a bike. It was a tough time for me, because we were poor. I had to walk miles every day, to get to my baseball games in the park, and to the mom and pop stores for baseball cards, and Old Dutch root beer. I had an old Red Flyer wagon which I used to load up with empty soda bottles, I found in the alleys. I cashed them in for pop and ice cream. Sometimes I found some pretty good stuff in the alleys. One day I got lucky; I found a 24-inch Schwinn bicycle, with flat tires and bent rims. The seat and frame were in great shape. The handlebars were crooked, but could be straightened out, once the headset was loosened! I knew all the problems with the bike were minor, and were fixable. I put the bike in my wagon, and dragged it over to Myles' garage. He made a deal with me. If I cut his grass, and weeded his garden for two weeks, he would put new wheels on the bike and tune it up for me.

We shook hands and I went to pulling weeds, as he began to build my new bike. The bike was beautiful when he finished it. He gave me a small pouch of tools, so I could take care of it. I learned so much from this dear old man. He taught me about responsibility, and shared his knowledge with me. What a great gift he gave to a poor little boy from the neighborhood.

When the kids in the neighborhood saw my new bike, they couldn't believe it. I went from nothing to having one of the coolest bikes in our gang. Not only that, I gained the knowledge on how to fix bicycles. I learned that when you are a mechanic, you have a lot of friends! Sometimes I'd lock my door and draw the blinds in our house when I saw them coming! Myles has been dead for many years now, but he still lives in my heart, mind, and hands, when I fix a bike for one of the neighborhood kids.

***

MORE ON MECHANICS

When I started high school, I fell in love with cars, motorcycles, and girls. (Not necessarily in that order)! I worked with my buddies, who were lucky enough to have cars. We toiled in their garages in the evenings, and on weekends. We pulled engines, did valve and cylinder jobs, brake jobs, and replaced transmissions. The tools we didn't have for some jobs we rented from Warshawsky, the junkyard man on Archer Avenue. It all was a lot of fun. We put running lights under the wheel wells, and custom chrome exhaust pipes on these street rods. We polished em' and raked em' up. We put super-sized, fuel injected, four-barreled carburetors on the engines, and modified the hoods with air scoops. We toyed with custom rims, racing tires, heavy duty pressure plates, and tachometers. It seemed like everybody had a car in high school except me! It was like an instant replay of the grammar school situation with the bike. Once again, I learned by helping. This time my buddies were appreciative, and took me with them when we went out cruising. I had earned their respect, and I was one of the crew. Sometimes, they let me drive; usually when they were drunk, or stoned, or in the back seat with some horny girl. I finally got my hot-rod after my freshman year in college. I paid for it with my own money, the same way I paid for my college education. I've always been grateful that people taught me about tools, and how to fix things. A lot of my college friends had no clue about anything mechanical. A lot of my blue-collar buddies, from the old neighborhood, had no clue about college. Heeee! I am really lucky that I learned how to travel comfortably in both worlds!

***

YOU DESERVE A BREAK TODAY

You deserve a break today.
It's hard to find a way to live…
while souls are screaming.
You deserve a break today…
from automaton bimbos in strip clubs.
They deserve a break too…
while souls are screaming.
You deserve a break today…
Two double cheese, for two bucks,
fills the void for a short while,
while souls are screaming.
You deserve a break today.
A fresh twenty, instead of dirty, crumpled dollar bills…
stuffed in your G-string,
while souls are screaming.
You deserve a break today…
Not cheap hotels on the road,
while your mind is going through transitions…
Waiting for the sun to rise,
while souls are screaming.
You deserve a break today…
While you wait to draw your last breath…
a tear in the corner of your eye…
a moment of clarity…
while souls are screaming.

***

THE BARTENDER

The sun is his enemy, as he drives to the bar at ten-in-the-morning. He unlocks the door, and smells the stink. It's dark and damp in this hole. He closes the blinds so the sun won't come in, and turns on the artificial lights. Then he turns on the neon beer signs. He always shits at home, but on occasion has to go again in the lousy tavern facility. Today is one of those days. He damns his luck as he pulls up his pants. He is sweating from his hangover, and he has the runs. This pisses him off.

He comes out, wipes his face with a clean bar towel, and pours himself a double vodka in a highball glass. He tops it off with an ounce of orange juice, then down the hatch it goes. The God-damned fruit flies are back again. They live in the sweet liqueur bottles. They get in through the speed pourers. The customers pull them out of their drinks, with their dirty index-fingers. They rarely complain. Some of the drunks don't bother, and drink the whiskey down, fruit flies and all. They say, "Free protein", as they laugh, choke and cough emphysemically, enjoying their attempt at dark humor.

The bartender does all the morning work methodically... counting cash, weighing bottles, cutting fruit, re-stocking bottled beer, and speed racks. He barks orders at the bar boy, who has a wet brain. By noon, everything is ship-shape and to his liking. He is pleasantly high now, because his stomach has held down the clear liquid which makes his life somewhat more tolerable.

The regulars come in at their usual times. Between serving drinks, he reads the newspaper and watches TV. Sometimes a new body will show up. If they tip him, he is all smiles, and tends to their needs promptly. Once in a while, a new female bar-fly will make her appearance. Then, he turns on the charm. He might even pour her free drinks, if he thinks he might get laid. He is in his forties now and is losing his looks. He still thinks he is a ladies man. The night man comes in at 6:00 p.m., so he begins cleaning up at 5:30 and stocks the bar, so his pal will have a nice clean bar to start out his shift. The bartender counts his tips, then heads home to shower, and eat some microwave dinner. He sits eating in his worn bathrobe, while watching one of those funky TV police shows. He shaves, and slaps on some cologne. He gets dressed, jumps in his beat up car, and goes bar-hopping.

He usually comes home between ten and midnight to pass out in his lumpy bed. He always sets his alarm clock for 8:00 a.m. Sometimes he stays out till the crack of dawn, if he meets a female drunk, who is attractive and willing. He used to get lucky all the time. Now, he only gets laid on rare occasions. He thinks his bad luck is due to more lesbianism in modern society. He says, "People don't have morals anymore".

***

COFFEE SHOPS

I like old fashioned coffee shops. You know the kind. The joints that have dilapidated furniture, and bad art on their walls. I love the raggedy old magazines, and the books strewn about the tables and floor. I sit in the stinky old sofas, or rickety chairs, holding my good old cup-a-joe. The radio is blaring jazz or blues, not that Starbuck's elevator music. I am in the company of construction workers, poets, artists, madmen, and the unemployed. I hate the antiseptic, upscale ways of the Starbucks chain. They don't allow 'real' artists to hang artwork on their walls. All they have is corporate, pre-approved prints...Yuck! Their coffee is too expensive for the rabble I like to commiserate with, but that's alright with me. I like a cheap cup of coffee. I like the old coffeehouses that sponsor poetry slams, and lousy folk guitar players. We try to hide our laughter when we hear a bad performance, which occurs almost every Friday night. We are in awe of performers, when they are actually good. We reward them all, good or bad, with tips and applause. Yah don't get that at Starbucks, baby! Do a test for me, will yah? Try and bring a harmonica in Starbucks, and do a few riffs. Do a Bob Dylan thing, like "Blowin' in the Wind". I bet the snotty manager will 'kindly' ask you to leave the premises. It's a mortal sin to disturb the corporate types masturbating their Mac-lap-top keyboards. The upscale mommies, with their sleeping babies in the thousand buck perambulators, might take offense at your disturbing song. It's not politically or socially correct. Up your arse' I say!

I like the conversations and arguments I hear in the mom and pop type coffee shops. Strong, cheap caffeine, and the sharing of ideas, stimulates my mind. In my favorite coffee shop, appropriately named the "Funky Java", I can play a game of Backgammon or Chess. I can fiddle around with an electric guitar or a set of drums. My 'shitty' art work hangs on the walls, along with the work of other 'not so great artists'. I sell a piece, every now and then. The owner's Mom is a 'neato revolutionary', who praises the working man, and just so happened to get herself a degree from Stanford University, way back in the good old days, when women weren't supposed to be educated. She is 80 years old and still likes her cocktails! She loves books, and art…a true intellectual, God bless her!

Starbucks won't have my art. I am the Anti-Christ to them. Lord help the world, if I should hammer a nail into one of their pristine walls. My painting might fall and hit some corporate attorney in the head. Lawsuits would fly! The corporates who run good old Starbucks wouldn't want this horror! Next time you visit the local Starbucks mausoleum, take a look at the plastic people. Most of these automatons sipping their lattes are totally self-absorbed. I'd like to bring my boom box in there, and play some Bo-Diddley for these anal retentive yuppies! I'd want to get some conversations or arguments going on! Maybe I would throw a few decks of cards on the sterile tables. Anything, just anything, to bring out some humanity in these robots. The whole scenario would end with me kicking and screaming, as the local gendarmes loaded me into the squad car, with my hands cuffed behind my back. "Watch your head, sir".

***

TYRONE

I first saw the man last year in my gym. He had a striking presence. He was a huge black man, wearing combat boots and gym shorts, with giant arms hanging out of a sleeveless, cut-off sweatshirt. He had a black nylon do-rag on his head, to keep the sweat out of his eyes. It was the crack of dawn, and we pretty much shared the huge weight room together. We made limited eye contact, and pretty much ignored each other. Out of the corner of my eye, I saw him doing dumbbell bench presses with 100lbs. in each of his huge hands. He had to be 6' 2" tall, and weigh about 265 lbs. I guessed his age at somewhere in the mid 50's, maybe a little younger. He was SCARY!…He was a mean looking man. I felt uncomfortable around him.

Our paths crossed every morning for three or four days. I respected how hard he worked those weights. Finally, I summoned up the courage to smile at him, and say hello. I figured the worst he could do, would be to ignore me. To my surprise he smiled wide and put out one of those big mitts, with the leather weight lifting glove on it, for me to shake. My hand disappeared in his, and a friendship began which I value to this very day.

He told me he was a retired Navy man. He used to box at Chicago's Windy City Gym, in the days when Muhammad Ali trained there. He was a personal fitness trainer now. He made a few bucks doing this, to go along with his pension money.

Tyrone taught me how to train, and what to take to ease my sore old muscles. He gave me an analgesic he picked up from Hines Hospital, which really helped ease my sore shoulders. He taught me to do a good soak in the hot tub, before I started lifting, to loosen everything up in my body. Tyrone and I did between 4 and 5 hours in the gym together every day. We cheered each other on to heavier weights, and more repetitions. We trained together for a long time...almost a year.

One day I took him to lunch, then back to my house to show him my art studio. I introduced him to my wife Debbie, and she loved him as much as I did right from the start. She called him a "Teddy-Bear", and that's what he was. He is one of the nicest guys I have ever met in my life. Tyrone is one of God's miracles in my life. He is always there for me when I need him. He is my brother. I didn't see him for a couple of months, because I had some surgeries done. He was out in Las Vegas, helping his mom settle into a retirement home.

He came up to me in the gym about a month ago, while I was doing my aerobic workout on a treadmill. We both smiled, and hugged. We filled each other up with information about what we had been up to during the interim we hadn't seen each other. All was good once again. I told Tyrone, "Go sneak up and put your arm around Debbie, she's sitting at the computer table." "I want to see her reaction when she sees your smiling face!"

So, Tyrone giggles as he goes off to freak out my wife. He puts his big, black arm around her little shoulders, and she grabs him and kisses him on the cheek. I walk over, toweling off, and the three of us talk about everything under the sun.

We parted, all of us joyful, feeling a lot of good will. The rest of my day was wonderful, because I was glad my good friend was back in town again. Tyrone still laughs when I tell him about my fear, when I first saw him. Tyrone said, "Rich, we are all God's creatures". "He put you and me together, because of his infinite wisdom". "There is no reason to be afraid of me, my brother." AMEN

***

PROFESSIONAL BASEBALL

Every morning in the spring, I start a ritual of checking the box scores and standings of my beloved Chicago White Sox. I also check the other team in town. They have a nauseating name, "the Cubbies". The anemic-pencil-necks, who live on the North-Side of Chicago, lovingly call them by this moniker.

I rarely watch baseball games. They are too slow for me, and I get bored easily. Watching baseball is like watching turtles screwing. I hate the outcomes of these games as well. I yell and cheer for three hours, only to have the South-Side-hit men get whooped in the final innings of the game. This really pisses me off! I realize that I have just wasted three hours of my life. I could have taken a nap, for crying out loud!

Football has always been more fun. Violence occurs on every play, and I don't care if my Chicago Bears lose, as long as they physically kick the shit out of the other team.

Modern day baseball players are overpaid and they whine all the time. The "corporates" own all the good seats in the ball park. Guys like me get nose bleeds from sitting in the upper deck or way out in the bleachers. It still costs me a couple-of-hundred bucks to bring my gnarly old ass, and a starry-eyed kid out to the ball game.

I make it a rule, never to watch my team if they are doing well. For some odd reason when I watch the games, I jinx them. Today, I started watching the Cubs and Sox play, in the "Cross-Town-Classic". The game was played in beautiful Wrigley Field. I had my Chicago beef sandwich, a bottle of pop, a bowl of fruit, and some veggies on my end table. The screen door was open, a gentle breeze blowing inside the house to cool me off. The sun was shining. My big ass was snug in my leather lazy boy chair, and my feet were comfortable on my favorite pillow. The White Sox took an early lead. My belly was full, and all was well until the seventh inning, when all hell broke loose!

The Cubs hit two back-to-back home runs to tie up the game at 3 apiece. I shut the damned TV set off, and went off mumbling to myself, cleaning up dishes, and tinkering with things, the way old men do. It started raining, so I sat down to write this story. When I finished, I tuned in to the six-o'clock news. They found a five-foot alligator in the Chicago River, and oh yeah, the Cubs beat the White Sox with a homer in the ninth inning. The final score was 4 to 3. I told yah! Baseball is a waste of time. I can't wait for the Bears pre-season games in August. Baseball sucks!

***

CARNIVALS

The smell of popcorn and perspiration...Sweet smells of cotton candy...Customers pass the booths, and smell onions, hot-dogs, barbeque, and cheap perfume. This is the carnival. Alcoholic roadie-hillbillies, smell of booze. They stand at their posts with jail house tattoos, red-eyed and dirty. They take tickets for the tilt-a-whirl, with greasy hands showing the dirt under their finger nails. They ogle all the giggling, baby, teen-aged girls, who are just starting to pop some breasts. This is the carnival, abundant with wild-assed teenagers walking arm-in-arm. He wears a leather jacket, and sports a greasy duck-tail hairdo that went out of style in the 50's. It's 90 degrees tonight. She proudly wears tight, hip-hugger shorts. She has pounds of cheap pancake makeup on her acne-scarred face. Her white belly and pierced navel hang over the top of her jeans, straining to blow the button clear off...like a bullet. Run for cover! She has heavy eye makeup, and too much lipstick on her lips. Her hair is sprayed stiff, just like the cotton candy.

This is the carnival.

People with no money to spare play the confidence games. "One more try, and you're gonna' win', "I can feel it", the carnie says. "This is your lucky day!" The proud father walks off with a garish looking plush animal worth less than five bucks. No mind that it cost him a twenty to win. It's for the kid, by God! "Nothing is too good for my kid!"...This is the carnival.

People drinking cheap beer and wine, smoking joints in the parking lots. They go on the rides, they puke behind the generator trailer...They never make it to the blue-plastic-Johnny-on-the-Spot. No-one saw them anyway. "Screw em' if they did!" The insane line up for another draft beer...This is the carnival.

Rock and roll is on the center stage...Electric guitars and huge sound systems are screeching and blaring, like a wounded animal. Strobe, colored lights, and fog machines, add to the strangeness of the night. Sulfur burns everyone's lungs, the left overs from the 'awesome' fireworks display...People are camped, and cramped on the lawn, with moldy old blankets. They are beds for teenagers dry-humping each other. People are in cheap chairs bought from Walmart, or just plain sitting or laying in the grass or dirt, like farm animals. The music is much too loud. Feedback comes from the guitars, as young men cum in their pants. Check one...check two...check...check...

This is the carnival.

They all go back home, really late. They go to the factory job with a hangover in the morning. The gas, electric, and cable TV bills are still laying on the breakfast table, unopened for three weeks...amidst other clutter.

This is the carnival.

***

BUTCHIE

He grew up on the North-Side of Chicago. He was a wild kid. He wasn't much for school. In high school in the early 60's he wore black t-shirts, leather jackets, and his 'cocks-comb' was blonde hair, greased in a pompadour, a ducktail in the back. He liked working on cars. He had a 440-Dodge-Charger, Hurst-Hemi, with a four-on-the-floor. When it started snowing, he frightened the teenaged girls who were in his car by doing donuts in parking lots. They loved every minute of the ride, after it was over. He was a wiry guy. Skinny as a rail, but muscled. Nobody messed with Butchie. Surprisingly, he was well liked. The fact of the matter was, he had a heart of gold beneath his somewhat menacing exterior. He helped little old ladies across the street, and didn't like the tough guys messing with weaker kids. Butchie drank beer, drag raced his car, got into some minor altercations with the law, but nothing really serious.

He rolled his smokes up into one of the sleeves of his t-shirt, exposing his tattoo of a hula dancer, or some other funky thing. Lord knows, I can't remember for sure. When Viet-Nam got underway, Butchie was drafted and saw some heavy action as a grunt Marine in the infantry. He took some shrapnel in his buttocks and was discharged honorably with a Purple Heart. Butchie is my wife's Stepbrother. They lost touch over the years, but by some fluke, or stroke of luck, she found his son and asked the boy if Butchie was his father. The boy gave

Debbie his old man's phone number. So Butchie, and his wife Sue, came to visit us in our home on Christmas Eve.

I really didn't know what to expect, and to tell you the truth, I really wasn't looking forward to meeting him. The doorbell rang and in comes this man in his 50's with a big pot belly, bill cap, and the biggest box of Italian cookies and pastries, I had ever seen in my life! He had a big smile on his face, a sweet charming wife, and he pumped my hand vigorously. He hugged my wife. It was a beautiful thing to watch. They both had tears in their eyes.

Butchie had a job as an over-the-road truck driver. He was an ace mechanic as well. He was an avid outdoorsman, who liked to fish and hunt. He lived in a trailer park, and owned a big old Hummer. I laughed so hard about this strange dichotomy that I was crying. We talked about muscle cars, and the old drive-ins in Chicago where we used to drag race. We talked about high school, and the dances we used to attend. He knew all the local Chicago bands from those days, like the Buckinghams, the Cryin' Shames, the Missing Links, and the Mob. It was three-in-the-morning before Debbie and Sue could get us to stop reminiscing, get Butchie out the door, and me up to bed. I can't remember a Christmas Eve, that I enjoyed more than this one. Neither of us drank or smoked anymore. I guess we both had done enough of that for three lifetimes.

After meeting that evening, we got together to hear a couple of rock-and-roll bands, and for a couple of barbeques at his trailer. We took them out to a Western-style steakhouse where Butchie and I consumed large amounts of red meat, corn on the cob, and baked potatoes. He showed off his Hummer to me that night. I loved the damned thing. This event occurred around four years ago, when gas prices were still manageable.

We haven't seen them since. It's a shame. I gotta' get my ass in gear, and reach out to them for good times, once again. I have to renew this friendship. Life is too short to lose a connection with great people like Butchie and Sue.

***

LABORING

Laborers have it rough. I know, because I did it for a long time. I remember the first time I had to break concrete with a 90 lb. jackhammer. I worked a shift in 90 degree heat, with a hard hat on my head, and ear plugs jammed firmly in my ears. I was seventeen years old. I ate limestone dust all day long. We didn't bother wearing a protective mask to protect our lungs from the dust in the 60's. The guys asked me how I felt at the end of the day. I told them that I 'felt great'. I think they all knew, how sore I was going to feel in the morning. That night, my arms and lower back ached so badly, I could hardly sleep. I took a bunch of aspirin, and as the agony subsided, I nodded off to dreamland.

The next morning, I was so sore, I had trouble raising my arms to eat my bacon and eggs, and drink my coffee. My dad was laughing at me. When I got to work, the men got a big kick out of me. They knew how I was going to feel. I carried planks and foundation wall forms that day. While I was a laborer, I shoveled shit, pulled nails, hauled concrete in Georgia buggies, and cut pipe with a concrete saw. I dragged compressor hose, cleaned debris from clogged pumps, and stood waist high in dirty water on many a day. I have to smile when I think of laboring; it is good work for a young man to experience. I'm glad I was young, strong, and tan. It was my day in the sun, so to speak. I'd give anything now, to be able to do it once again. On second thought, writing suits me just fine now!

***

FUNERAL HOMES AND MY FINAL PARTY

They look so beautiful inside. The flowers smell sweet. The coffee room has a wonderful aroma as well. You get to eat great cookies and nice little sandwiches. Girls are all dressed up in their finery. I get to check out their legs and ample breasts! I guess that's why they call them FUNeral homes!

This is how I viewed these wonderful places to honor the dead, as a young man. I only had to bow my head for a minute, and pretend to pray, as I looked at the cold, dead, body in the expensive receptacle called a casket. I thought, "Their troubles are over now." Then I'd jump up, making the sign of the cross, and run across the street to the local tavern, to drink whiskey and pick up girls. After all, I had a nice suit and tie on, and a guy has to shoot while the ducks are flying! I delivered flowers for my brother for 50 years, God bless his soul. I know how to set up funeral baskets in the big end casket urns, and grace the caskets with funeral scarves. I met the directors and the guys who worked on the bodies. Most of them had a good sense of humor. A man couldn't have a dark, morose personality in this type of business. A small percentage of them developed a depressed state of mind, from the job. They either drank too much, 'went cuckoo', or the worst case scenario I suppose, ended up with the gun in their mouth. As I grew older, and wiser, my outlook on Funeral Homes changed. I had a little more respect for the people being laid out. The Funeral Home business is a rip-off. A good funeral and wake with the flowers, prayer cards, mass, organist, singer, headstones, plots, casket, and luncheon will cost you around 15 or 20 grand these days. Whew! I know, because my brother and I set the whole thing up for my elderly mom. I remember the casket viewing room. I felt like I was buying a new car. All the caskets have these fancy names, and features. I tried to inject a little humor into this depressing shopping experience. I asked the funeral director, if he had a casket with red and yellow flames on the side of it for my mom.

My brother Jim, gave me that angry, "Oh my God" look. I knew I blew it. Anyhow, we took care of the whole deal, and got our contracts that day. Little did I know that Jim would end up in one of those caskets a couple of years later, after Mom died.

These funeral affairs are barbaric, medieval, religious, social rituals. I hate them. I want to be cremated. I want my jug of ashes to be decorated with a skull and crossbones. I want the jug to have psychedelic colors. I want the urn with my ashes to sit on a bar, in some local gin-mill. I want all my friends and relatives to get good and drunk that night. I want all the young ones to meet up for trysts in local motel rooms after the party. I would laugh like hell if one of the drunks at my funeral party, knocked over my urn of ashes, and it broke on the bar room floor! It would be a scream seeing the little Mexican bar boy trying to sweep up my ashes into a to-go, foam food receptacle. Maybe he will slip in a cup of coleslaw, just to be kind!

I want hard rock music at my wake. I especially would like the music of Jim Morrison and the Doors...also Janis Joplin, Jimi Hendrix, and the Grateful Dead. This is the background music I request for myself, dear Debbie, please make a note of it! I want the paintings I have done over the years, hanging on the walls. I want pictures of me drinking scotch, with young babes at my gallery openings. I want these on a big board, on an easel. I also want pictures of me with my wife, daughter, mom and dad, my brother and sister, all the members of my extended family as well. I want to be decked out in a leather vest, a Harley-Davidson t-shirt showing the tattoos on my dead white arms, before they turn me into a 'crispy critter'.

I want a cheap, old, pine casket, the crummiest one, the bottom of the line. I don't want flowers. Send your money to a children's hospital or buy your wife a new hat instead. At my funeral mass, I want them to play Elvis singing, "If I can Dream". There wont be a dry eye in the house! Try not to cry for me...If I did you wrong and didn't make an amends, please forgive me. Sometimes, in my life, I was a real asshole! I want you all to remember one thing. I had one hell of a life! As my old man used to say, "I went around twice"! I sure love you all, and want to stay, but we all have to face this day. Just remember to always have fun and don't hurt anyone. It's going to be one hell of a party! I wish I could be there to enjoy it with you all! I think the Great Spirit has other plans for me. I look forward to the 'other side'. I picture Jane Mansfield on a barstool to my left. Marilyn Monroe is on the barstool to my right. They are both whispering "sweet nothings" in my ears, while Ava Gardner is sitting in my lap! I'm smoking a Marlboro Red and drinking Chivas Regal on the rocks. Roy Orbison is singing in the background on the jukebox. Ah, now this is heaven!...I put my drink down and start sweating...A horrible thought strikes me...I think, "There will be hell to pay, when my wife Debbie gets here"!

***

CREATIVE BLOCK

I can't paint...I can't write.
My mind has gone south baby...
I ate my calorie allowance for the day.
I think I'll take a nap.
I could go out, and get a sun tan, or watch a movie on
TV...
This bores me to no end...
I think I'll take a nap.
How many words are left in me?
Will the mighty pen deny me, like the paintbrush has?
Will I end up watching court TV shows, or Jerry
Springer?
Will I take up knitting?...
I think I'll take a nap.
Somehow, I must work through this thing.
I must search for more variety in life...It's all out there...
It's got to be in my head...somewhere.
It's mine for the taking if I can only see...but,
I think I'll take a nap.
Will my muse come back to me, or will I be jilted by her?
I feel like an empty vessel.
I feel as if I have been abandoned by my sexy lover.
She promised me fame, and fortune.
The bitch went to live with some younger writer.
That's it! Screw that damned whore!

She abandoned this old man.
I'll get even with her.
I'm going to take a nap!

**

INTERNET CHAT ROOMS

There exists a mind-boggling variety of chat rooms on the internet. There's a chat room for bikers, the artist's café, the metaphysics room, the millionaire's club room, the gardening room, and the author's lounge…There's a philosophy room, a religious fundamentalist's chat room, political chat, sports chat, and sex chat…The list goes on and on…forever!

You would think, that with all the diversity available, a person could learn a lot of awesome information, meet new and interesting friends, and broaden their horizons. WRONG!… For example, If you have America Online, go into the artist's café. See how many people are actually discussing art. I'll bet you five bucks that you can sit there and observe the chat for half an hour, and maybe, just maybe,…if you're lucky, you might see one or two sentences remotely related to art. Most of the banter will be about politics, sex, baby formulas, more sex, relationships, rock stars, sex between rock stars, recipes, or other banal subject material. If you introduce yourself as a working professional artist with credentials, an interesting art web-site and a great sales history, you might get a few people to say hello to you, but then amazingly, they revert back to, and continue on with their ridiculous babble.

I've observed this phenomena, over and over again, in many chat rooms. Sex seems to be the favorite discussion topic, no matter what room you go to…excluding the religious fundamentalist's room…(sometimes however, a foul-mouthed agent of Lucifer will appear even here, but will usually be ejected by the room's watchdog…and reported to AOL). I don't think I would ever want to enter a room titled: "I love you Jesus". I do however, respect their right to maintain this room, and I believe the conversation should be ONLY, about their love for Jesus. Sex rooms even deviate from the topic at hand, although they seem to be the most honest about sticking to speaking about the fetish they advertise, with their room's title. In every room I visit, there are posers and "wannabe's". People are mostly full of shit. Many of them are down right mean. Some of them spend hours every day, in their room of choice…It is a form of mental illness. Geez! Get a real life, not a virtual one!

When I drank alcoholically years ago, I spent a few hours every day in these chat rooms. I was 'buzzed' and it was a nice diversion for me. I didn't have to think about my real life, and what a mess I had made of it. Maybe that's why these people sit at their keyboards day after day, night after night. They want to forget the realities in their lives. They can pose as the people they really want to be. Day after day, year after year, they twaddle away their precious time. They are wired into a new addiction. They embrace a new unreality in their lives. Chat rooms are just another excuse to procrastinate, and flounder in mediocrity. It's a sad and lonely world out there in Cyberspace. For many, it's better than the "real world" we have right now.

***

WE WERE THE BAD BOYS

We hung in packs, like wolves. There were always eight or ten of us…sometimes more. We were south-side Chicago, working class dudes. It was the 60's. We claimed our territory, the entire west side of Marquette Park, Chicago. Guys sometimes tried to come from other neighborhoods to 'rumble' with us. We never backed down, and they never came back. We went to teen hops together. We found safety in numbers. We never went to the bathrooms alone. It was too unsafe to go anywhere alone at a dance. You might get 'jacked up'. At the dances, we carried half-pints of whiskey in our suit jackets. We slugged them down in the parking lots or in the 'john'. We used to call the half-pints, 'half-dogs'. I think my old buddy Russ, invented this strange colloquial reference. We dated the girls who 'put-out'. These are the type of girls who wore heavy eye makeup, short skirts and push-up bras. We took them to the Double-Drive-In outdoor movie theatre to see 'grind house' features. You know the type of films,…wild bikers, vampires, undead zombies eating human flesh…good movies for making out and grabbing ass. We steamed up the car windows, and copped free feels. Sometimes a guy hit a home run with one of these bimbos. We learned to live hard and fast at an early age. After the drive-in movie, we took out dates to the White Castle hamburger joint on 71st St. and Western Avenue for twelve cent hamburgers and greasy French fries. Before we took them home, we brought them to Marquette Park, for more making out, until the Chicago Police threw us out of there. We sat on park benches, after the sun went down. We smoked cigarettes, and drank cheap wine. We passed the bottles around. 71st St. was a block from our park benches, in the playground. It was dark where we roosted. We could see the Chicago Police squads parking under the street lights, if they chose to come by and roust us. Behind us was grass and trees. We could see squad cars in back of us in the park, if they decided to hem us in. They had to run a couple of blocks from either side to get us. We were young and could always out run those fat donut-eaters. We had our escape routes all planed out way ahead of time. We ran through the alleys before they could catch us, and hid out in a garage owned by one of the guys. We drank beer from his old man's fridge. We promised to replace the beer, but never did. He always got his ass kicked by his dad, but was a stand up kind of guy and never ratted us out. We eventually paid him back in 'spades'. Half of us died in car wrecks, from drug or alcohol abuse, or the Viet-Nam war before we were twenty-five years old. Most of us had our share of divorces, shitty low paying jobs, and heartache. Some of us actually went on to wealth, trophy wives, and country club memberships. A few of us still get together and talk about the old days. We all have physical problems in varying degrees. Most of us have given up the booze, and the smokes. I still feel the swagger, and loyalty when we sit down to eat together. We all share the illusion that we are still the baddest guys in the joint. I know it's all bullshit, but I still love every minute of it. I'd always take a bullet to protect anyone, from the old gang. You see, we are Marquette Park guys. We hail from the South-side of Chicago...Enough said.

***

I NEED A PIECE

My wife says I watched too many violent movies in my life. I'm a firm believer in the National Rifle Association. I grieve the passing of the great Charlton Heston. I think Michael Moore types are pretentious, dough boy liberals, who speak from both sides of their mouths. I love Ted Nugent and spaghetti westerns. I like all kinds of shoot-em' up movies. I am a staunch believer in the second amendment. I have a legal right to bear arms, because I am a citizen of the United States of America. This right is guaranteed to me by our great Constitution.

My logic tells me that since I'm getting a bit elderly, a nice handgun might even the odds for me someday; if some vandal decides to enter my domicile to knock the old geezers off, and steal our possessions. A nice Glock, or police special, might fit the bill for me. I don't want any of these gang-bangers moving into my neighborhood, to come into my house at night, and try to steal my social security check.

Debbie says I'd probably end up shooting her, myself, her sister, or our daughter. She also thinks it's possible that I might shoot myself, just loading the darned thing. Deb says there is no way she is going to keep living here, if I buy a weapon. She says that the older I get, the more I act like a teen-aged boy. Am I losing my mind? Has adult-onset-dementia taken over my cognitive reasoning powers? I think not. I'm going to buy my cherished weapon, and hide it in a safe place. She'll never know. I can take it to the firing range, and make new friends! The only thing that worries me is more hearing loss. I don't wear my damned hearing aids anyway. I'm gonna' buy it! I can't wait to stand in front of the mirror and pretend I'm Robert DeNiro, in *Taxi Driver.* "You talkin' to me?" Alright!

***

THE DVD WARS: A TUTORIAL FOR MEN

There is an ongoing war between husbands and wives... boyfriends and girlfriends...males and females, when they visit the local video store to rent movies. Since all men are dogs, and are visually stimulated by images of female nudity, and graphic violence, they are immediately drawn to the DVD jackets which display these types of enticements. Women on the other hand, are romantics. They are drawn to droll, little, slice-of-life type films. These are mindless romantic comedies, musicals, or three-hankie movies that make them weep. male-bashing type chick-flicks are also in vogue today. These movies invariably put men to sleep. I find myself snoring in my chair after ten minutes of viewing, drooling down my chin. My wife keeps jabbing me in the ribs, telling me what a great movie I am missing...Sure.

Now that the dichotomy is presented...You men, who are reading this chapter can well understand what I mean by the title of this little ditty. I want Rambo, she wants the Phantom of the Opera. Who do you think is going to win this war? In my house, where I am lord and master, my wife always wins. She threatens to go upstairs and watch Masterpiece Theatre, while I am watching Rambo single-handedly blow up every yellow skinned man, woman, and child who doesn't stand for truth, justice, and the American way. I've tried watching my movie without guilt. I end up sheepishly going upstairs, apologizing for my rudeness, with my head hanging down like a guilty schoolboy. I show her my sad eyes, and crawl into bed with her. I try to decipher the mumblings of the English actors. My wife kindly puts on the closed captioning for me. In ten minutes, I am snoring. My wife gives me a shot to the ribs, and tells me I better go back downstairs. I'm happy, and refreshed from my little snooze. I made amends to my wife. I proceed to dish up a giant soup bowlful of ice cream, grab a bag of peanut butter cups, a bottle of water, and go back to the Rambo movie. See guys, I got my way! It was a tough war tonight, but I'm a tough soldier just like my hero, Rambo.

At other times, I have to succumb to the chick-flicks. I try and laugh in all the right places. I get up and go to the bathroom a lot to splash cold water on my face, so I don't fall asleep. My wife keeps asking me if I'm enjoying the movie. I keep saying, "Yes honey, you really picked a winner this time!" A smart husband, or boyfriend learns how to lie convincingly!

The video wars are very much like clothes shopping. For all you men who are reading this, remember one thing: If your wife or girlfriend ever asks you, "Does this dress make me look too fat?", Always tell them, "Are you kidding honey, you're beautiful and slim in that dress!" "It makes you look as sexy as the first day we met!" She will prod you more by saying, "Do you really mean it, or are you lying?" Even if she looks like Tugboat Annie in a sausage casing, lie through your teeth, men! If you do all these things exactly as I have instructed, you will win most of the wars! Always remember, the bigger the lie, the larger the payoff! One last thing men, be careful! Women are dangerous, unpredictable, cunning, and smarter than you! Think before you speak!

***

THE ZEN OF PLANNING A DAUGHTER'S WEDDING

I meditate every morning, while I am on the treadmill at my gym. I blank everything out of my mind, and transcend reality until a 20-or-30-something female, in a skin tight spandex outfit, comes within my peripheral vision. I say, "Many apologies, Great Spirit, the material world has ensnared my evil mind once again."

There is a Zen to everything in life. Zen is the Eastern philosophy of living in the now, going with the flow, seeing the whole, and chilling out the western mind which wants quick answers, and tends to prioritize and compartmentalize just about everything.

Recently, my sweet daughter Catherine received an engagement ring. She has been seeing this nice young man for approximately three years. I loved his respect for tradition. He came to our home, before he proposed marriage to my daughter. He asked my wife and I, if he could ask Catherine for her hand in marriage. How sweet! I was so proud of him! Finally, my daughter would have a fine husband, and I would have a totally acceptable son-in-law.

The wheels immediately started to turn. The mothers of the bride and groom, along with my daughter began the 'holy quest',...for dresses, wedding gowns, flowers, invitations, bridal gift registries, string quartets, restaurants...ad infinitum. My Zen mind told me this so-called quest involved huge amounts of money. Red lights and sirens went off in my head, telling me to block everything out! I reasoned that all the decisions these women made, would change at least 20 times until it got close to wedding-day crunch time. My future son-in-law and his dad displayed great male intelligence by going fishing way up in Northern Canada. They solved their problem of listening to all this female tittering, in a quick, decisive, male kind of way. God, I admire their chutzpah! I was left here, all alone, to deal with all the elaborate female machinations. Surprisingly, the women told me very little. I guess my wife and daughter knew how I would react, if and when I heard about all the costs involved in the event. All was being done secretly, in a Machiavellian way, behind my back. Female subterfuge always prevails. I had the creeps! The goose flesh appeared on my arms, and the hair stood up on the back of my neck. I knew things were happening, that might freak me out!

I was shown an iphone picture of the wedding gown. It was a sight to behold! Beautiful pearls and lace adorned the garment. My little girl looked like a queen. Her waist was waspish. She was thin, and beautiful, thanks to countless hours of working out at the gym, and meals from Jenny Craig. My daughter looked just like a fashion model! I then made a huge mistake. I asked my wife and daughter a simple question: "How much?" Immediately, as if rehearsed, in unison they responded: "You don't need to know!" "It's none of your business!" Hmmm. I had visions of me in my future years, sitting in my urine-soaked wheelchair, enjoying my lunch, a nice can of Rival dog food, and stale saltine crackers. My daughter and her husband would be frolicking at their vacation home in Cabo San Lucas, while I was staring mindlessly at some institutional wall, painted an ugly green. Snow would be blowing outside my little barred window. I shook my head and dispelled these notions immediately! My heart was pounding, and my hands were sweating. I needed to do my 'mantra'. I needed to dispel all unnecessary thoughts. I started deep-breathing exercises, and in my mind, envisioned a beautiful field filled with flowers. My blood pressure started coming back down into a comfort zone. "These are merely father-of-the-bride panic attacks," I reasoned.

I have to remember how fortunate I am. I remember how grateful I was when the doctor handed me my baby girl for the first time. She was healthy and beautiful. She had all her pink little toes, and fingers. She worked hard in all her endeavors. She overcame great obstacles in her young life. She will finish her senior year at DePaul University this year with honors. My sweet wife, and daughter, have to be first priorities in my life, if I am to have meaning. I guess I can wait till I'm sixty-two to buy the new Harley Davidson Road King. We'll see what my wife and daughter have to say about that! Keep your fingers crossed for me!

***

THE COMIC

He travels a lot for gigs.
Marriage, for him, is out of the question.
His art is a fine obsession...
It's all to make the people laugh.
He practices facial expressions for hours...in front of
bathroom mirrors,
In seedy motel rooms...he writes monologues with verve,
no gloom...
He likes to light up a room with his material...
For you see...he is a comic.
He answers the hecklers, without showing fear.
He counters their barbs with put downs so clear...
He brings the house down.
The house doesn't see his angst, and sweat...
Pre-show jitters are always a threat...
He forges ahead without a regret...
For he knows he is a comic.
Sometimes he enters silent clubs.
No one is there, that is the rub...
He gives his all...He pretends, he is playing, Carnegie
Hall.
He knows, there will be nights like this...
Getting drunk on stage, with nowhere to piss...
The nights he bombs are the worst...
His jokes are dead, his mind in a hearse...

Clawing, and scratching, to get out of his grave...
Joke after joke, will not save, the comic.
Year after year, success is more fleeting...
Age creeping up, he's taking a beating.
No money saved, no 401K, he sees only darkness, a potter's field grave.
Alone in his room, after the show...
There's always the whiskey, the whores, and the blow...
He'll ride the wave till it crashes down...
Leaving him a sad, old clown.
He did it for the people, you know.
Night after night, he brought them his show...
Making them laugh, while on a roll...
He was a comic.
Now he eats hamburger, rather than steak...
The crowds aren't there now, it must be his fate...
He never gave up, he always stayed true...
He did it for me, he did it for you.

***

THE SINGLE MOM

She had a strong, dominant mother, whom she loved very much. No father ever entered the picture of her life. Her mother told her never to be afraid of boys. Her mom always told her, "You hold the power, not them". The daughter traveled a lot in her job, and had a lot of affairs with men in many different cities. All she wanted was a child to love. She never wanted a man. She finally received what she wanted… her glorious pregnancy. Unfortunately, she had a miscarriage. By a strange twist of fate, she found a man who loved her. She adored him. She had a child born of passion. After a short while, she abandoned the husband. He had a proclivity for drink and outside women. She was crestfallen, but she was a woman of means. She was independent financially and emotionally.

The world would belong to her and the baby. She wanted her baby boy to live in a special world, a world of her own design. He was her passion. He became her magic prince. Her little boy was her fantasy world, where everything was perfect. In essence, he became her dreams, fulfilled.

She taught him spontaneity, and creativity. No psychological hang-ups, or walls were to clutter his perfect mind. She feigned normalcy, and conformity, when confronting the outside world. She cultivated an ego-oriented child. She held him separate from the other children. He became her God. The other children were his minions. However, he lacked social skill with the other children. He suffered greatly when he tried to relate to them. They called him a "mama's boy". Her asked his mother, why he didn't have a father. She never answered him adequately. She continued to design a perverse, fairy tale world, for him. Naturally, he recoiled and rebelled. In high school, she couldn't control him anymore. He resented her for the sham she had put over on him. He realized how mentally ill she was, and hated her for it. She withdrew more and more, into fantasy. Life was a cruel joke for her, without him. He broke her heart. He dated girls, and abandoned her. He left home at the age of sixteen. She died inside of her soul. Her son had finally realized, how much damage she had done to him, with her suffocating love.

The years passed. Therapy for him, and loneliness for her. She lived in filth. She saw no one. In her broken mind, she created the world she once had, with her little son. She played it over and over again in her twisted mind. Finally, her neighbors became concerned. The once beautiful home she had maintained, was in disarray. Grass and weeds grew wildly in her yard. Garbage was thrown in her driveway. Public health officials were called. They entered, and found her living in her own excrement, and discarded carry-out food containers. Flies and maggots ruled her domain now. Her loving son, hadn't visited or called her for decades. She had been abandoned by her little prince. She died alone in a public nursing home. He never came to visit her. He never attended her wake or funeral. He never has visited her grave. He gladly accepted the money she left to him, in her will. A mother's love knows no bounds.

***

YOU HAVE THIS CONDITION

Roll out the red carpet once again...Line either side with accordion players...It's time for them to play the dance macabre...Have nubile young virgins in shear gowns throwing rose petals ahead of you, as you make your way to the check-in desk of ambulatory services. Tell the mindless hospital employee at the desk who you are, and what you are there for. Tell her, "I have this condition".

Put on that God-damned hospital gown, for yet, another time. Your wrinkled ass hangs out the back, the ties are designed to pull your arms out of your aching arthritic arm sockets. Do they purposely plan to humiliate patients, with this ridiculous gown? I say, "Hey nurse, can you tie up this damned thing for me', "You see, I have this condition."

It all starts out with one little problem. You are fifty-five years old, male, beat up from 33 years of construction work, booze, and cigarettes. You wanted to press on till you were sixty-two, but your body denied you this opportunity. You tried to keep working in agony, for a couple of months, but ended up at your union hall applying for an early retirement pension. You explain to the secretary there, "I have this condition".

Little by little, piece by piece, your body falls apart. Every year comes another surgery. You take another pill, which creates other problems, in another area of your body. When the family doctor isn't sure, he sends you to a specialist. He covers his ass. He doesn't need a lawsuit. His medical malpractice insurance is high enough. He says to you, "You'd better see the Hematologist this time". You need a specialist. You see, "You have this condition".

Your eyes eventually lose their youthful sparkle. Once erect, your proud walk turns into a hunched over, elderly shuffle. They systematically de-humanize, categorize and over medicate your tortured body and mind. You have to take care of "your condition".

What if you never gave up the whiskey you loved so much? What if you kept smoking those wonderful cigarettes? Do you remember that sweet rush of nicotine, filling your emphysemic lungs, after a few good belts of scotch? You were happy! You didn't care. You had no 'freaking' condition. If you hadn't sobered up, quit the cigs, and the all night carousing, maybe you wouldn't have "your condition".

Maybe your damn body just rebelled, when you took all the joys away. Maybe you'd still be healthy if you hadn't gone the way of the hospital machine. You dispel these insane thoughts immediately. You reaffirm your decision to get healthy and do what all the doctors want you to do. You rationalize that you might have died a horrible death years ago, if you hadn't changed your lifestyle.

But, somewhere in the corner of your mind there still exists the old self. Here lives the risk-taker…the exciting guy you used to be. He is the guy you love, who lived life with reckless abandon! You miss this guy…Your old rugged self. You keep him jailed, in the corner of your mind. You live a bland existence now. It bores the hell out of you. Life isn't as sweet as it used to be, because of "your condition".

You envy guys your age who never saw a doctor. These are the guys who drink, and smoke, right up to the end. They are the lucky ones, who keel over with massive heart attacks…the lucky ones who are dead as a mackerel, before they hit the ground! They didn't know what hit them. They never suffered or worried. They never knew they had "a condition".

***

RICHIE-ROBIN-AND ME

Richie the Polack was a good friend of mine. I met him on a tunnel job years ago, way back in the mid-70's. He was running a crane, I was running a loader. Being young guys, we both loved to run our mouths. We bullshit, told tall tales, chased women, and drank a lot of booze together in dive taverns. We liked each other, and sealed our friendship over a million shots-and-beers.

After the job was over, we parted ways for a few years and then ran into each other once again, on another tunnel job. Richie ran a pipe-jack machine. He was in the drop shaft where they lowered 42-inch concrete pipe. He ran the machine that jacked this pipe into the tunnel, after we mined out the clay. I 'lived' way up in the heading where the clay was mined by a young hillbilly guy named Robin....I lay on my stomach or on my side on a battery powered dinky, which motored a couple of cars filled with clay, out to the drop shaft. When crazy Robin was mining, I was under the conveyor belt sharing hits on a joint he had rolled...We laughed all day long. When the cars were filled up, and I was out in the drop shaft...the big crane sent the hooks down...and Richie and I hooked up the full cars to be emptied...We threw stuff at each other, and yakked it up while the cars were being unloaded, topside. Richie and I joked around, or showed each other pictures from men's magazines...anything to pass the time...waiting for the empties to come back down. After work, the three of us went to Lyons, Illinois, notorious for its' corruption and B-girls. We picked a new den of iniquity to drink in every night. There was a whole mess of em' in the spectrum. Richie, Robin and I were the Three Musketeers.

Now, here comes the hilarious part of this story. Whenever Robin and I hit a big old rock we couldn't mine, we'd have to bring in a Bosch electric drill, dynamite, and anywhere from 300 to 600 ft. of electric cord. Robin and I would drill and shoot the big rock, then we'd yell for Richie to pull out the electric cord. Robin and I had a grip on the cord while we were yelling, "Richie, pull it out, you fat ass!" "C'mon now, we aint got all day!" We'd hear him groaning, swearing and muttering to himself. Robin and I would look at each other, tears running down our cheeks, trying to muffle our laughter.

Robin would continue to yell, "Get your fat ass in this tunnel, and find out where it's caught!', We don't have all day, we need to start mining again!" Richie was a big man, and he would lumber in all hunched over, sweating like a dog, gasping for breath. His back had to be killing him. As he got closer to us, he'd be swearing more and more. When he got up to where we were, he saw us laughing, smoking cigarettes, holding onto the electric cord. You can only imagine how pissed off he was! I'd have to pick up a big Crescent wrench, or clay spade to keep him away from us! He wanted to kill us both. It was great, insane, fun! He'd calm down after a couple of hours, than the three of us would go to some seedy bar, and all would be forgotten.

He'd forget about our trick, then in about a month or two, we would do it to him again. The neat thing about it all, was that sometimes, the cord was actually stuck under the railroad track. Poor Richie lost this game, no matter what!

One time, the three of us had a long weekend...4 days or so...We decided to go down to Robin's little house in East Indianapolis, Indiana. The Indy 500 was on that weekend. The 'tittie bars' were packed. Richie and I drove down there in my pickup truck, drinking beer, and smoking reefer, all the way. It was a beautiful day, and we listened to southern rock, or country music, enjoying the sunshine and fresh air. We got to Robins' house, and saw it was a dirt poor looking shack. It was real country, just like good old Robin! We met his barefoot wife, who was a real "looker". She chased their dirty, bare-assed kids all over the house. Robin fired up the grill, and fixed up some hamburgers and hot dogs for us. We drank cold beer, and Jack Daniel's bourbon straight from the bottle. At the same time, joints were passed all around. We all continued to party hardy!

The exhausted wife put the kids to bed at sundown, and Robin, Richie and me, sat up around a pit fire in the backyard. We talked about the job, about our adventures, and had a good-old time. We decided to turn in, set the alarm clock for the crack-of-dawn, because we were goin' fishin' the next day. We had lots of coffee, bacon and eggs, and toast, fixed by Robin's wife. We then iced the beer in the cooler and headed out to the lake. We didn't catch any fish, so we headed out to a western-style clothing store. I wanted to buy my 8 year old daughter some 'real' cowboy boots. They were expensive as hell, but I knew she'd love em'. That night, Robin took us on a trip to the best 'tittie bars' that East Indianapolis had to offer. Richie got really drunk, and we had to keep him cool. We were promptly thrown out of a few bars, because of his over-all belligerence. Finally we realized we were all going to end up in jail, if we didn't head for the 'high-country'. We went back to Robins' house, and built another fire. Richie snored like a wounded bear, sleeping while sitting straight up, in a lawn chair, beer in hand. Robin and I just loved the sight of the big-old-guy, looking like this.

The three of us did back-breaking work together for a couple of years. I loved every minute with these guys. I didn't hook up with Richie again till we were in our 50's. He had gotten fat, and old, just like me. He showed me a knife wound he had gotten in a bar fight. The guy stabbed him pretty darned good. He had a big chunk of flesh missing from his abdomen. He was lucky to be alive, from the looks of the wound. Richie had been sober for about five years, but he started drinking again on this job. The boss wanted me to take over his bulldozer, because Richie was drunk and couldn't handle the work. I wouldn't do it. I told the boss-man, that I never would fuck my buddy. The only way for me to sit in that dozer seat, was if Richie came up to me and said it was alright with him.

Richie did just that. I got the new dozer, and my old friend hung around for a week, till he hooked up with another job. He got in his old, beat up, powder blue pickup truck, and off he went. I haven't seen Richie or Robin for years now. I read in the union newspaper that Richie retired this year. God only knows where that good-hearted hillbilly, Robin ever ended up. By the way, my kid didn't like the fancy cowboy boots.

***

DARKNESS AND LIGHT

I'm learning to enjoy the darkness of the night…I like the quiet in my house. It's just me and my pen now…wondering what is going to come out of my mind. The birds are asleep now. I'm too deaf to hear the cricket's song anymore. The reality of my situation doesn't upset me. I've even gotten used to the ringing in my ears. The tinnitus doesn't bother me anymore. I think more about my mortality these days. I suppose this is normal for a fellow who isn't in the best of health. My friends are afflicted by illnesses in varying degrees. A lucky few are still enjoying perfect health, but their turn will come.

I enjoy sitting in the dark. I think of my little girl, years ago in bonnets and sun dresses. She wore shiny patent leather shoes, and pretty little frilly socks on her feet. She put her little arms around my neck, as I lifted her into her car seat, when we went to church on Sundays. My wife always looked beautiful on Sunday mornings. Usually, I wore a coat and tie. In the dark, I picture green fields, filled with wildflowers. Sometimes I walk out into the street to breathe fresh air, and gaze upward at the moon and stars. The dark is beginning to become my friend. The only time I am afraid of it is when I think I can own it. It exists of itself. It is too big for me to command. I must learn to accept it for what it is. I must give up attempts to understand it. I can find peace, this way, in the dark.

I say my prayers at night in the darkness. I don't pray for myself. I pray for others. I can't kneel down to say them anymore, because it's too painful for me. I don't think God minds. He knows that if I could kneel down, I would. I thank the Great Spirit for another day. I ask forgiveness for all my sins. I quit praying as a young man in college. I thought God was a myth. The whole concept of God was merely an opiate for the poor, uneducated masses. I believed I was above all that nonsense.

I began to pray again at the age of 53. It took me over thirty years, to begin once again. I was drunk, fat, and soaking wet; manacled to a jail-house wall. I had a spiritual awakening in jail. I saw who I had become. The fog in which I had been living, was lifted from me. I wondered, "How do I pray again, after thirty years of silence, and denial?" I don't know how I began, I just started doing it. I'm not a religious man. Rather, I'm a spiritual man. I embrace something greater than myself, because I gain the strength I need to survive adversity, from the powers outside of myself. I realized that I control nothing. This realization allowed the light to come into my life. Maybe true wisdom comes from embracing the darkness, and the light.

***

WAITING ROOMS

Thank goodness I decided to become a writer. I spend a lot of time in doctor's offices and hospital waiting rooms. All I have to do is bring my little notebook, and a couple of ballpoint pens, and BOOM!...The creative process can unfold!

When I was an artist, creating paintings, I sure couldn't bring my easel, water, brushes, paints, and canvas, into medical office areas. I don't think the medical establishment people would appreciate my artistic endeavors. Besides, by the time I got set up and got into the creative flow of painting a piece, my name would be called and I would have to bound off for the examination room. I'd be covered in paint. Everything else around me would be slobbered with my paint, including the carpeting. Painting in hospitals, or doctor's offices, is a total 'negatori', unless you are a kid in a children's hospital. Kids always should get carte-blanche for creativity!

These waiting rooms always have a TV, for the patients to enjoy. Somehow the sets are always tuned to shows which I totally deplore...Shows like "The View, Jerry Springer, the shopping channel, hideous children's cartoon shows, et all". The people on the 'tube' are chortling, and laughing. Their insanity depresses me. Don't they realize I'm waiting to have a colonoscopy, and endoscopy performed on me? It is not a happy time! I'm nervous, hungry, and have a headache, due to caffeine and food deprivation.

The magazine selections are as depressing to me as the TV shows. I have a selection consisting of, "Highlights for Kids, Better Homes and Gardens, People Magazine, Business Week, (which REALLY depresses me!), and a variety of health and doctor's magazines which always frighten me!" I ask myself, "Where the hell are Playboy, Maxim, Popular Mechanics, Rolling Stone, ART news, or the New York Times?" Oh well, at least I can write all this meaningless bullshit in my little notebook, while I'm waiting for my procedure.

I find myself daydreaming, wishing for a buxom blonde nurse, with large breasts and a short tight white skirt, wearing those luscious white nylons, and high heels, to escort me to pre-op, and a yummy drug cocktail! I start thinking of the girl who served my hot buffalo wings, at the local "Hooters" restaurant the other day, where Russ and I had lunch. She had a beautiful face, a lovely smile and a curvaceous body that could sink ships, man! In the middle of my daydream, my name is finally called out. The nurse who escorts me to my pre-op room is short, fat, and frowning at me, much in the same manner that sister Elizabeth scowled at me, in 6th grade Catholic grammar school. As she hands me my hospital gown and goody bag, I notice that her upper lip is in dire need of electrolysis. My wife bids me farewell, and I start freezing my ass off, waiting for the inevitable, while lying on the gurney. I lie there grimly, looking forward to the drug in the drip bag, which will somewhat reduce the pain I will experience, caused by the upcoming anal and oral indignities, which I must endure. I told the anesthesiologist that I require mega-doses of drugs, since I'm a recovering alcoholic. They always seem to short-change me in this regard. I go through agony during the procedure, and scream, more drugs guys! I told you so! As I leave confused, and drugged to the 'max', feeling violated, I hear the young, female receptionist say to me, "Have a good one". Hah! "You have a good one too, bitch!" I think all kinds of nasty things, as I'm wheeled out in my wheelchair, on my sore ass, my wife by my side. "Someday, this procedure will be experienced by you, sweet young thing!" "I hope you have a good one, too!"

***

ICE

She was cold and beautiful. Her smooth skin was ivory white. She had one crystal blue eye, the other eye had a haunting hazel color. Her thick black hair added to her mystique. It was silky smooth, and cut fashionably, cropped closely to her beautifully shaped head. She had a figure like Audrey Hepburn, not quite as frail, because she was muscular, with larger breasts and better-defined hips.

She loved dressing stylishly, in a very refined fashion. She loved the simple, clinging black cocktail dresses. She wore high heels, and always wore a single string of expensive pearls around her lovely neck. She never overstated her elegance. Artistic flair and style, in the way she dressed, and in the way she walked, was her signature.

Ice exuded sexuality and confidence. She epitomized every man's fantasy. She was poetry in motion. She spoke intelligently, and with authority. She was knowledgeable in both the arts and the sciences. She understood politics, as well as the stock market.

The men she competed with in the business world nicknamed her "Ice". They were intimidated by her. They were afraid to ask her for a date, because deep in their little boy hearts, they felt she was unapproachable. Her style and savoir-faire frightened all the men away. She was lonely. She tried various upscale dating services, and dining clubs for singles. She always walked away from these places disappointed.

At the age of 30, she gave up looking for men, and resigned herself to a solitary life. She pursued her hobbies, and developed friendships with a small group of women and men who were interesting, but she never found the romance she so desperately desired in her life. One day, in the high-rise office building where she worked, she dropped her purse while getting out of an elevator. The janitor of the building who was mopping the floor at the time, quickly picked it up for her.

She thanked him, as he smiled broadly and looked into her beautiful eyes and said, "What would you think if I asked you out to dinner tonight?" Amazingly, she heard herself saying, "I think it would be nice!" He was handsome, and she felt an immediate attraction to him. So after work, they went out. He took her to a not-so-fancy restaurant, but it had great food! They laughed and talked…He put her at ease by asking her if she wanted a beer. She laughed and said, "Why not!" He wasn't afraid of her, and was confident in himself. She adored him right away. Every date they had after that first night, was better than the one before. In a year, they were married. Her friends and colleagues were shocked. They felt that she had married beneath her station. "She could have done so much better," was the buzz.

Her janitor husband never felt the "deep-freeze" from Ice. He was her lover, friend, and confidant. Ice never had better sex or conversations in her life, until she met him. He was genuine, and honest. When the children came along, he quit his job, and stayed home to take care of them. He cooked and cleaned and was loved by his family, because he always put their interests ahead of his own. He was a valuable husband and father. Ice was the breadwinner, and she did well. She and her husband have been married for thirty years. They have three fine children, and two grandchildren. The husband calls Ice his "hot mama". She gladly gave up haute-cuisine and art galleries for hot-dogs and ballgames. In her wildest dreams, she never thought her life could ever be so wonderful! Sometimes, love is strange.

***

ROAD FEVER

I remember the good old days when four cars rushed to be the first, at 4-way stop signs. The guy who won went into a power slide, did a rolling stop, then gunned his accelerator pedal to the floor to claim his #1 position. The other three drivers gave him the middle-finger-salute, to acknowledge Mr. Speedy's expertise.

For some weird reason, the other drivers respected his aggressiveness and aplomb, in spite of a considerable lack of courtesy. The three drivers who were left sitting there gambled in much the same way. The stop sign was always negotiated quickly, and all drivers usually went on their merry ways, quickly and without accidents.

Today, this is not the case. The four drivers today, safely come to the stop sign and just sit there for what seems like an eternity. I'm usually the last one to arrive. Sometimes I wish I had a stopwatch to time this 'Mexican standoff'. I scratch my head, while I mutter every lousy swear word, that I have in my vocabulary. I watch these morons wave the go ahead sign to one another. They all still sit there, as if in a coma. If I gun my car to end the insanity, all three of these brain-dead individuals lurch at me with their vehicles. People just seem to be afraid to make a decision. Female, suburban, cell phone users, with their vans and a million crying kids inside of them, seem to be the absolute worst at the 4-way stops. Elderly people in Mercury Marquis, aren't much better.

Also, I love the driver who passes me at 90 miles an hour, just to cut in front of me, slow down, and do ten-miles-an-hour under the speed limit. This insane driving, defies all logic. I get myself worked up. I'm nervous and angry. My left eye starts twitching. My knuckles are white from squeezing the steering wheel. I pretend I have my hands around the neck of the offender. Calming music from Il Divo or Sade goes by the wayside. I wish I had an anti-anxiety pill to pop, but then I risk being pulled over by a 'county mountie' for driving under the influence.

I try not to drive too much anymore. Driving just burns up my life savings and retirement checks. It's too bad I have to drive to hospitals and doctor's offices. The only free rides are in the big ambulances, when you think you're gonna' have the 'big-one'. When I look at my taxes, I realize these really aren't free rides. I have to admit to the fact that too many little things bother me. Sometimes it takes a little pain and fear to get a realistic look at the big picture!

***

ONE MAN'S FOXHOLE PRAYERS

Dear Lord, Please don't let my wife find the black lace thong which I left in my Armani suit jacket." "She says she is going to the dry cleaner's this morning, and I promise from the bottom of my heart, from this day forth, to always be faithful to her." This my friends is forever to be known as a foxhole prayer. Soldiers in fierce battles always used these prayers, when they thought they were going to die...Later on when they survived the battles, they forgot about God, (as we all do sometimes)...The soldiers went back to their prior habits of drinking, whoring, and stealing...It's human nature to sin! Anyway, back to the story. The husband who just said this prayer is hurrying home from the local Dunkin' Donuts. He is breaking every traffic law known to mankind. He has coffee, milk, juice, and a dozen donuts for 'the little woman' and his kids. He pulls into the driveway, flies into the house like a bat out of hell, leaving the car door wide open. He slams the donuts, and beverages on the kitchen table and runs up the stairs, (3 at a time), into the master bedroom where the suit jacket is lying with other clothing items, which are designated for the morning delivery. The husband shuts his eyes, says one more quick prayer, and proceeds to dig into the suit jacket pocket to find the black-lace thong. He shoves it deeply into the pocket of his jeans, and looks furtively in both directions. He breathes a deep sigh of relief, and prepares to greet his wife, who is taking a shower. NOW, HE WILL KNOW IF SHE

FOUND HIM OUT! "Good morning honey", he sheepishly says in his good-boy voice. She responds by saying, "Hi, sweetie, did you get the donuts?" He replies, "Yes honey- buns, I got your favorites, because I'm so much in love with you!"

"Whew", he thinks, "I dodged a big bullet, aimed straight for my heart this time!" They both go downstairs and the kids say, "Daddy left the car door open Mommy." "He looked like someone was chasing him when he ran up the stairs!" Dad recovers quickly and lies by saying, "I thought I was going to pee in my pants, so I used the other bathroom while you were showering." The whole family laughs, as Dad runs out to the car to lock the lace-thong in the glove box, and close the doors of his car.

As the family enjoys the donuts, the Father thinks, "Wow, I still have a super quick mind, and all moves." "I'm the man!" As he's sipping his coffee, a horrible thought enters his mind. He hopes the motel he and his mistress used the other night doesn't send any discount miles, or coupons to his house. He is never the first one to check the mail! More prayers are in order. The moral to the story is, "Never allow a corner of your rose garden to have a weed patch in it." If you live clean and morally, you never have to fear something gaining on you, when you look over your shoulder. Remember, cheaters never prosper!

***

LOVE AND SEX, AMERICAN STYLE

The mythology promulgated by various fundamentalist religious organizations in America presupposes the unity of one man, and one woman in holy matrimony, FOR LIFE. Wow! Life can be a long sentence if you pick the wrong woman. We in America promise to love, honor, and obey, till death do us part. Frightening eh?

Come on now. Get real! Are you going to live up to these expectations? No way Jose! Like any other red-blooded American male, your job is to see how much you can get away with, while still staying within the graces of your sweet little wife. A real man tries to go to as many taverns, gentlemen's clubs, card games, sporting events, fishing and hunting weekends with the "boys," as he can possibly manage. You have to put your stamp of utter male dominance on the marriage, as soon as possible. This is a process taught to newlywed young males by old-timers, who have been married for many years. The old man pulls the newlywed prospect aside and says, "You've got to break-em' in right away son." They're just like horses...you gotta' ride-em' and break-em' or else they'll be useless to yah!" "Remember, there's only one lord and master in your house, and by God it's you!" "Don't ever forget it, sonny boy!"

This is the 'so-called' wisdom of the ages, being passed down from father to son, from uncle to nephew, and from every "swingin' dick" in the bars or on construction sites throughout America. Somehow in practice, this advice never works. The women rebel and rule with tears, recriminations, silence, shopping sprees, and last but not least, the withholding of sexual favors! Some women will even take you to divorce court, and fleece your unfaithful ass! EEEEK! Now that's the last straw!

We are too hung up about extramarital affairs in this country. When a guy or gal is caught in the throes of passion with another individual, other than the sacred marriage partner, all hell breaks loose. The knowledge of betrayal, is too much for the recipient of this undeserved lack of loyalty. We in America all go through divorce, annulments, alimony, and child support. If the marriage isn't dissolved, a grudge is carried and utilized whenever necessary, on the unfaithful partner. This grudge lasts till the end of his-her life! Sheesh! All of this happens because of a little tête-à-tête. A one night stand...A chance for a little variety and adventure in our otherwise humdrum work-a-day lives. I don't get it.

In Europe, people are calmer and more logical about these affairs of the heart. They accept the extramarital affair, as a part of life. They calculate the proper times for infidelity. They try and be discreet. The major difference is that the betrayal is more easily forgiven. Husbands, and wives are both having affairs. They still seem to maintain a loving marriage, and raise healthy, happy, children. Their rationale more readily seems to accept human weakness. People are allowed to be passionate outside of marriage once in a while. Somehow, the Europeans seem psychologically healthier than their American counterparts. Physically, they are more fit than their American counterparts, as well.

Maybe the reason for fitness, is to stay more attractive for the opposite sex. Also, the Europeans don't have to comfort themselves with excessive food, and booze when the "blush" evaporates from their marital beds. In Europe, a little sexual variety probably helps people maintain a good sex life with their life partners. Here in America I see an epidemic of sexually deprived, morbidly obese individuals. I really don't think most of these people are 'getting it on,' other than with a few super-sized sandwiches or extra large order of greasy fries. They wash it all down with a Big Gulp drink. Ahhhh! It's better than an orgasm! We have plenty of pornography here, but I think most Americans who look at it, do it alone. What a sad state of affairs! No pun intended.

We as a nation are sexually starved. We have too many baseball games for the kids, pressure on the job, bills to pay, and deadlines to meet. Most young married men and women in their prime, just don't have the time to have sex. America has always been a nation that works. Too bad we forgot about screwing. Ah, my mind still lives in the 60's. I still buy Playboy Magazine. Shoot me for being a pervert! My liberal sexual attitude is a healthier place for me to be, until my wife and daughter read this episode! You know me girls, I'm just bullshitting! Gulp!

***

THE OLD RECORD SHOP

Jimmie owned the place. I loved the guy. He was a recovering heroin addict, 30 years younger than me. In Chicago southside terminology, He had 'chops'. He was cool, and he had knowledge of all types of music. He always had some great 'jams' playing in the store. Buddy Miles, Bo Diddley, Miles Davis, Chico Hamilton, Sarah Vaughan, you name it and he had it. He sold nothing but the old vinyl LP's. Cassettes and CD's just don't give you the sound of the old wax LP's.

Jimmie bought the shop from a retired Chicago police officer. I went in there usually 2 or 3 times a week, to watch them play chess and drink strong black coffee. Eventually, I would saunter through endless aisles of the old thirty-three-and-a-third LP's. I found such gems as Susanna McCorkle, Milt Jackson, the Jimmie Hall Quintet, John Coltrane, and Muddy Waters. I always left the shop with 2 or 3 records, in pretty good condition. The price for a record was anywhere from 2 to 7 bucks...Not a bad deal! It was amazing. I figured out how to hook up a nice turntable to my Bose stereo system. It wasn't easy, till I got an alligator clip to ground the turntable. I contacted Bose, and they shipped the accessory to me for only ten bucks. The sounds were wonderful, and worth the wait.

Jimmy and I talked a lot about sobriety, when his policeman friend wasn't there. I respected his anonymity, and he respected mine. He had a nice young girl friend who watched the store for him, when he was taking classes at the local college, or out buying records. Jimmie let me hang my paintings in his shop. They hung there for a couple of years, but I never sold a piece. I hung one of Jimi Hendrix, one of Janis Joplin, and one of Jim Morrison. Later on at a National Art Show, the Hendrix painting won a minor award. News of my painting sale, appeared in the local newspapers, and we hung the article in the record shop. I sold the Hendrix piece to a guy who drove a truck for a living. Anyhow, Jimmie started slipping again. Business wasn't very good, and he was going to have to close his record shop. He started snorting heroin once again. Heroin is a cruel mistress. His girlfriend confided in me, and told me of his plight. She cried a lot of tears in the days to come. She knew I loved Jimmie, and shared her angst with me. I asked if I could help in any way, but she told me he was too far gone. I kept coming to the shop, but the doors were usually closed. The only times the record shop was open, was when Jimmie's girlfriend could work a shift. She had her own full time gig at a hair salon. After a while, I saw him again. He had sallow skin, and dark circles under his sunken eyes. He had lost a lot of weight, and looked like a ghost. He smiled at me, put his arm around my shoulder, and told me everything was fine. I told him I knew different. He was off and running with the horse again, and you can't stop a runaway train, so I didn't pitch sobriety to him. I knew he didn't want to hear that from me anyway.

I caught him packing up his records, the week he was closing the shop. He said, "Hey man, you've been a great friend and customer', "Why don't you grab 3 or 4 records that you like." "I'm moving back to the city." I said, "Are you sure you want to part with them Jim?" He said, "Yeah man, its OK." "I don't have room for all of them anyway." Then he asked me if I could spare him some cash…I gave him a couple of twenties.

I knew where the money was going to go, but I gave it to him anyway.

I saw the girlfriend a few months later. Jimmie and she weren't an item anymore. He sold all the records for 'junk' and was 'spiking' in some desolate building. He was sharing needles with other addicts, somewhere in the inner city. I had to write his story. I couldn't believe such a smart kid could do this to himself; but we all initially think we are smart enough to handle our addictions. I think he might have died. I think that was the news I heard on the street, but I blocked it all out of my mind. I didn't want to remember him this way. I sure miss that kid.

***

ARTISTS AND WRITERS

Artists and writers are a difficult subject for me to write about. These two groups contain a total spectrum of head-cases, and mostly self-absorbed non-doers. I know this to be a fact, because I have congress with many of these creative types. One of the differences between me and 90% of my brethren is the simple fact that I actually work to promote and sell my work. I actually have my stories published, which I put to paper with my trusty ball point pen. A lot of these people are more talented than me. They just don't know how to follow through. They are a queer lot. I'm not saying what I produce is very good. Value is always up to criticism. However, I always step up to the plate, even if I keep striking out. For example, I joined a creative writer's group a year ago, because I thought it was a wonderful opportunity to learn the craft. I was sorely mistaken. These people whined about how their talents were being ignored. Most of the whiners just want to smoke reefer and drink Jack Daniels. Art and writing was just an excuse for them to be boorish and unruly. I asked the lot of them what they had published. All I was presented with was 'rag-tag' folders of cheaply printed garbage. Some of the material was very good, but most of it was crap. I presented them with a nicely bound 350 page Memoir. I worked 800 hours on my book, which was my first effort. None of these so-called writers bothered to look at it. My autobiography took me seven months to write and edit. I worked 8 hours a day. I edited, re-edited, then hired a professional editor to proofread and correct punctuation errors for me. I edited more after he was through, and corrected 40 mistakes. I found more mistakes after I had it published, but it was a good effort. It was mine, and I was proud of it.

Writers that don't publish are either lazy, or just posing as writers. Most of them love their status as misunderstood victims of society. I never met so many cry babies in my life. I quit the group after the second meeting. The thing which really blew my mind was that I was only at the craft of writing for 8 months and already had a book on Amazon.com...These people had been doing their work for 5, 10, or 20 years, and had nothing to show for it. Go figure that one out! These are so-called educated people. I don't know about all that 'crapola', I'm just a retired bulldozer operator.

Most artists also lack good business sense. I recently quit an artist's co-operative, run by a man who insulted me constantly. The fellow insulted my friends, and customers as well. He made a $1500 sale very difficult for one of my best clients. He wanted her paintings to hang for two months, and didn't want to take a check from her. GAWD! Hey dude, wake up, take the money and run! Hang something else on the wall. Hang your dirty underwear on the gallery wall, if you have to! I don't care! The guy had delusions of grandeur, in his roach infested little storefront gallery. He said to me, "This co-operative is about the art, not you and your book!" Huh? Sales are sales, and the more I promote myself with newspaper articles about me, my book, and my art work...the more money I make. People are attracted to ME, in this specific gallery. People like to 'buy' the artist. If the director of the co-operative, and the artists in the gallery have no media history or resume to speak of, shame on them! I decided to quit the gallery after this horrible fiasco. I emailed an established art gallery owner, with triple the space, in a luxurious setting. She immediately took me and my artwork onboard. She knew I was a good businessman, and that I knew how to paint and sell my art. I understood her clientele, and the target market in which she was interested.

I tried to explain to the co-operative members how to operate a gallery, but they chose to speak, rather than to learn and listen. Selling art isn't about drinking Jack Daniels bourbon. Art openings entail looking for sales opportunities, and keeping your eyes open. You are there to inform the art buyer, and to be helpful. The way I see it, and have always seen it, is to 'promote thyself'. If artists felt this way in a co-operative, we all could prosper together. There is no place for trivial rules against promotion of any sort. All promotion is good promotion. The green-eyed monster of envy and jealousy ruins many a gallery.

Oh well—it's their loss, not mine. I have been through this before. No bad words were exchanged. I'm above all that nonsense now. Let them notice the empty chair, and my lack of dues at the next meeting. Maybe they all will think this old curmudgeon has finally passed away! None of them read or write anything of merit, so I won't have to worry about what I've said about them in this book!

***

HE BECAME MY HERO

I was feeling sorry for myself. The blood thinners I have been taking for my peripheral artery disease weren't doing a good job of getting rid of a blood clot. That evening I happened to tune into the local news on TV, and saw something which I never will forget. An eight year old boy is playing catch with Nick Swisher of the Chicago White Sox. The kid is throwing hard, and right on target. What amazed me, is that he is standing on only one leg. The missing leg was taken by cancer.

This endearing young man plays the position of catcher on his little league team. Can you imagine the pain involved in crouching down for 9 innings with two good legs? This great kid does the job with one. What he had to learn about balance and performance, through trial and error, is truly incredible. It surely humbled me. This kid inspires me. When he swings his bat and gets a hit, he hops quickly to first base.

God shows me these things all the time. He puts heroes right in front of my eyes, and shows me what a lucky guy I am. I heard that since Swisher hung a picture of the little boy in his locker at White Sox Park, he has been on a huge hitting streak.

Before he met the kid, he was batting an anemic 232. For the last 19 games he has been batting 469. We all need heroes in our lives. Nick Swisher and I were lucky enough to find our hero. He is a little 8 year old boy, braver than any man I have ever known…a cancer survivor and a winner.

So, whenever I am feeling sorry for myself, I take a trip to the local hospital or nursing home. I ask to volunteer. I ask if I can make the rounds. There are many heroes for me to meet in wheel chairs. I listen to their stories. I bring a cheap stuffed animal, or a jig-saw puzzle. I spend a couple of bucks, and a couple of hours of my time. The payback from my investment of a little time, is nothing short of phenomenal.

***

MY AMERICA

I love you, and your big sprawling diversity. You are argumentative, mean, and loving, all at the same time. America, you are my home town. I love you because you know how to party on the 4th of July. You are all about hot dogs, fireworks, rock and roll, and cheap beer. You embrace all of us, rich and poor. You are not perfect, but somehow you make it all work. People are dying to get in here, to become American citizens. We are still the greatest country in the world. We work more hours than anybody in the world, and with more pride. We are proud of you, America. You always find a way. You overcome insurmountable odds, to defeat what seems to lead us to certain failure. You are resilient, and alive. Don't count us out, or tread on our flag. Here's to the black, white, yellow, and brown citizens, the rainbow of America. Here's to the cowboy, drill rigger, field hand, and waitress. Here's to the crack-pots, poets, inventors, and people who never quit. Here's to the wealthy, who look for a way to give their money away to the best causes. Here's to the men and women in our armed forces. Thanks to the people who march for peace, and those who protect the environment. Thanks to those who are always looking for a way to keep America strong.

Let's raise our glasses high to the pros and the cons. We have the freedom to speak our minds around here. Don't take away our right to bear arms. Don't mess with the United States Constitution. Let's not get lazy now. It's time to show the world we are still the best. These times test our mettle. In these trying times, people who believe in themselves and our way of life, are going to find ways to prosper. Hard work, and persistence will allow us to grow. I won't give up on my country. I will adapt to find new paths, to travel to prosperity once again. I refuse to listen to the naysayers. We Americans are as tough as nails. We always find a way.

***

CELL PHONES

The year was 2004. I couldn't wait to get one of these new-fangled gadgets into my hot-little-hands. I begged my wife for months to buy us a couple of these wonderful cell phones. Lo and behold, one Saturday after I came home from work, she presented me with my precious Samsung. I immediately started speed reading the instruction manual, absorbing about 30% of the information, before I started haphazardly diddling around with the mechanism.

I chose my ring tone, a somewhat conservative and non-obtrusive sound. I didn't want to disturb people with ridiculous songs emanating from my cell phone. Also by designating a song, I might share too much information with complete strangers about what kind of guy I was. I went about storing all the important personal and business phone numbers, which I would need in my travels away from home. I'll never forget when my cell phone rang for the first time. I was speeding down a four lane highway, at about 70 miles per hour. I proceeded to freak-out, and drop the damned phone under my accelerator pedal. I quickly slowed down and stuck my head underneath the dashboard to retrieve it. When I lifted my head, I saw the rear end of a brand new Cadillac, coming up on me real fast! I simultaneously slammed on my brakes, and hit the send button on the phone to receive my call. Thankfully, I didn't slam into the Caddie, but I lost my call. The phones mechanical sounding female voice said to me, "If you want to hear your messages, enter your password, and then press the pound sign." Huh?

So much for that...Debbie, my wife, never told me what my secret password was, so I had to call her at work to get it. I'm scribbling it down quickly with one hand, while steering the car with the other. I don't have my bifocals on, so my prescription sunglasses are pulled all the way down to the tip of my nose, so I can see what I'm writing. Once I start dialing, in order to see the teeny-weeny numbers on the phone, I have to extend my arm way out. I'm dialing with my hands, and steering with my knees. Of course I'm in rush hour traffic now.

I finally dial in all the correct numbers. The mechanical voice gives me a new instruction this time. She says, "You have one saved message." I manipulate the buttons to 'saved messages', and see a big, fat "0". How could they do this to me? I will never know who wanted to call me! This is horrible! Here is a new device which is supposed to simplify my life, and it has caused me nothing but angst on the very first day I've used it. Welcome to the world of senseless multi-tasking.

Cell phones used by other people bother me just as much as my own. They constantly invade my privacy. I had one extremely rude woman carrying on a conversation with her business partner in a nice restaurant. She had one of those speaker phones, and it was turned on full blast, while my wife and I were trying to enjoy our dinner. I mean to tell you, this thing was as loud as the public address system at a professional sporting event. I never saw my wife more pissed off in my entire life. Debbie got up and kindly asked the woman to turn the phone off. The nice lady gave my wife the finger, and told her to mind her own business. Before Debbie got a chance to grab this woman around the throat, and shut off her air supply,

I quickly jumped up to fetch the manager. He immediately put an end to the problem for us. The other diners gave us a round of applause, as the rotund, red-faced, business woman left in a huff. I noticed she didn't tip her server, and this made me dislike her even more.

I tell people not to call me on my cell phone anymore. I hate the choppy conversations, the missed signals, and the utter lunacy of it all. The damned thing over complicates my life. It's a horrible toy! The cell phone turned on me. Yet, I still keep it, and pay the extravagant bill. It's nice to have if I am stranded somewhere with a car that doesn't operate properly. It also is nice to have after some gang-bangers have robbed, and beaten me within an inch of my life. All I have to do is pull my glasses down to the tip of my nose, and dial 911 with my bloody fingertip. In all other cases, cell phones are just another pain in my ass.

I remember my mom and dad's, good-old-fashioned, black, rotary dial telephone from the Western Electric company. I think I dropped that big old 'sucker' a million times in grammar, and high school. It never broke! The thing was indestructible! We didn't need cell phones in the 50's and 60's. Life was lived at a slower pace back then. Once a man came home from work, his day was over. He sat in his favorite chair after dinner, and lit up a nice Camel cigarette, while his sweet little wife mixed up a nice pitcher of martinis. My dad hugged my mom as they sipped their drinks. If the phone rang, he used to say, "Don't answer it Irene, I'm busy watching Perry Como." He figured if it was something important, whoever called would try again later. Dad took another deep drag off his cigarette, and smiled. My father always told me, "A man's home is his castle." He was right. Back in those idyllic days, he had it made.

***

MANTRA OF A SELFISH AND ANGRY MAN

I don't want to get along...Stick political correctness up your ass...

I hate all the political candidates...In fact I hate a lot of people...

I guess I don't want to get along...I don't want you people to bother me anymore...

Leave me alone.

Don't call me at dinner time, or on Sunday...

I'm not buying it anyway...I want to be left alone.

I shouldn't harbor anger or resentments...

I'm told they are the poisons that I take, to kill my enemy...

Bullshit! I like getting angry!

Turn the other cheek?...Once, twice, never thrice is my battle cry.

Some antagonistic bastards need a good ass-whooping.

People smile, try to do good works, and the end result is always the same...

They get played...They get whacked...they get attacked.

It just isn't fair...I don't want to get along...

You see I have ideas...I know how things should work... in my life.

Just let me be...I won't mess with you, till you mess with me!

I don't want to get along, until you have something that I need.

***

THE COP

He was a smart enough kid,...Irish-Catholic from the South-side of Chicago. He went to Catholic high school, then on to college. He graduated with a degree in Criminology, then on to a series of horse shit jobs. The times were not good. Finally, he took the police exam for the City of Chicago. He passed with flying colors. They didn't take him. He blamed it all on affirmative action, and lack of "clout". He took it again, and did even better. This time they called him in for his physical, and a battery of psychological tests. They did background checks, interviews, and more testing in every area imaginable. Finally, he was admitted to the Police Training Academy.

He was proud, and so was his family. He went through rigorous physical and mental conditioning. He graduated at the top of his class and celebrated with his cronies, in the Irish bars on Western Avenue. He was a rookie beat cop now, in the Englewood neighborhood. He was told it was shit duty. He loved the adrenaline rush of it all.

Pimps, whores, drug dealers, confidence men, psychos, rabid animals, puke, roaches, gunfire, insults, threats, domestic altercations, street gangs, and running into places, where no sane white man would ever go. This was his life. He learned how the system worked. He learned the numbers, the bag pick-ups, who to roust, and who to leave alone. He learned how to watch his back, and the back of his partner. He earned respect from the department, and from the people on the street.

He learned how to deal with his fears, angers, and frustrations. He drank whiskey, smoked cigarettes, and shook down good looking whores for blowjobs, while he drank his coffee, parked in dark alleyways. The violence of the street life turned him inward. He eventually acquired a whiskey-nose and a potbelly.

He bought a nice home, raised five beautiful children, along with his lovely wife, who dutifully listened to him. He went to mass every Sunday at the Catholic church. He took his kids to little league games, and ballet lessons. He went to picnics and affairs with other police officers, and their families. He was a member of the special brotherhood of the Chicago Police Department.

His wife and kids never knew the disgusting things he did to himself, and others. He swore, drank to excess, and bullied people. He stole, tortured, and strong-armed people. This street life he learned, turned him into an animal, no better than the low-life criminals he arrested. In some twisted, perverted way, he loved every minute of it. Sometimes, when he came home drunk and fell into bed, he started crying. He wailed like a banshee sometimes, locked in the bathroom with a bottle of whiskey, a pack of smokes and his loaded service revolver. He didn't want to wake the wife. The kids were grown and gone, by this time. The wife and he were empty nesters now. He thought how easy it would be for him, to stick the gun in his mouth and pull the trigger, but that was the coward's way out.

He would never do that to himself, and his family. Better to die with honor, without the mortal sin of suicide on his tortured soul. He worked drugs, then homicide. He saw just about everything a man could see. It all was dirty, inhumane, and gut-wrenching. After 35 years, he took a desk job, but still yearned for the action of the streets. He hated pushing papers around, and filing reports. He retired after a year. He was amazed he had survived the job. Now, he has the diseases of an alcoholic cop…Emphysema, high blood pressure, obesity, and arthritis. He continued to smoke and drink. He saw too much of the dark side in his life. He took his wife to Mass and Holy Communion every Sunday. Somehow, this gave him a modicum of peace in his tortured soul. He begged for forgiveness, when he said his prayers at night. He still loved his wife, with his whole heart and soul. He enjoyed seeing his successful children; and enjoyed playing with his grandkids. They gave him great joy. Sometimes when he was alone, he still had the crying jags. Life wasn't the same without the action of being out on the streets.

He's an old man now…He hopes against hope, that God has forgiven him for his sins. In his heart, he still keeps his dark secrets. He sits in the tavern every afternoon where cops congregate. He tells the rookies about the good old days. They all laugh in amazement, about the things he did, and got away with in his career.

He goes home, and the lonely feeling creeps back into his mind. His wife sees the emptiness in his tired eyes. She knows better than to ask him about what is bothering him. He just waits, and looks at the clock. He marks days off the calendar. He sits in his home in the kitchen, or on a raggedy old bar stool, looking out the window. He is marking time now, waiting to die.

***

NEW HOME SHOPPING WITH MY WIFE

My wife convinced me last Saturday, to go shopping for a new home. This adventure usually consumes the entire day. It makes her happy. She tells me, "I have to have something to dream about." We never buy anything during these escapades. You see, I've been down this road many times before.

My dreams consist of thick sandwiches, girls jogging down the beach in slow motion wearing skimpy, Baywatch-type bikinis, or Chicago Bears linebackers putting crunching hits on opposing quarterbacks, during N.F.L season games. Feed me, give me a couple of video rental movies featuring sex and violence, point me in the direction of my lazy-boy chair, and I'm a happy camper.

Women are more complex. They look at these new homes with a microscope. They talk about things like upgrades, tile, cabinets, extra sun rooms, basements and taxes. My wife makes me walk up and down all the stairs of these model homes with my battered legs, and after a couple of hours, I'm ready to throw in the towel. I say, "Hey, when are we gonna' eat?" My wife gives me a look of incredulity, and says, "We have two more stops to make before you get to feed that stomach of yours." I think she is excessively cruel!...After all it's Saturday, for God's sake! Amazingly, on this shopping trip, I find the house of my dreams. There is no basement to afflict our elderly legs. The home is beautiful and spacious, inside and out. The upgrades are lovely.

The rear of the home faces a gorgeous lake, with a gazebo and an asphalt running path which goes all the way around it, for lovely evening walks. The fitness center and concrete swimming pool are just a stone's throw from the backyard. The community is a 55-and-older enclave, with a 24 hour security car, which dutifully patrols the area. The association fees cover the grass cutting, snow plowing, and all outside repairs to the home. The fees are reasonable, and the taxes are manageable. The home is priced within our budget. I'm hot to put our town home up for sale, and buy this house, RIGHT NOW! My wife looks at me and says, "Are you crazy!??"

She continues, "I wont be close to my sister, or my best friend Louise,' also I have an extra 20 minutes to drive to work." "We have to worry about paying for Catherine's last year of college, and her upcoming wedding is August of next year!" I think, "Why in the hell did you take me shopping?" Man, the air quickly emptied out of my happy husband balloon. I thought we were shopping for a new home? What the hell is this chicken shit attitude all about? We have the dough, let's roll the dice! I'm 59 years old, with a good credit rating, and more than a few bucks in the bank. I own my own town home, and I can get a 30-year-fixed mortgage. I can slap down a nice fat sum on the new home, and we will live happily ever after! One thing I like is that a geezer like me can get a 30 year fixed mortgage. They can't discriminate against me because of my age. Heeee...like I'm going to live to be 90, with all of my health problems! So who cares? Let's rock and roll! Also, we own both our cars and all the stuff in our house. I have no credit card debt. GEEZ, Debbie, it's a 'no-brainer'!!!

Wifey says I should be more realistic! I hang my head like a six-year-old child, and kick the dirt. I'm sweaty and hot, and my legs are worn out. Even my underarm deodorant isn't working anymore. I've been had again! Debbie then saves the day. She says, "Let's go to the steakhouse, and get ourselves a couple of those thick rib-eyes that you love so much." "We can get loaded, cheesy-baked-potatoes, and a rich gooey desert!" "Then we can rent a couple of movies…You can pick them out!" I say, "Alright!" All is well once again in my life! We sing old Beatles songs, on the way back to our neighborhood. My sweet wife looks lovingly into my eyes and says, "Thanks honey for taking me home shopping." "Now, I have something to dream about." I don't get it, but I know one thing; my dreams were fulfilled that night! I got to watch "man type" movies with a full belly, and my arms around the woman I love!

***

ANIMAL LOVERS AND OTHER STRANGE PHENOMENA

To me, owning one animal, who is well behaved, is allowable. Having two is pushing the envelope. Owning three or more is insane. My wife and I go to this couples house on occasion, and I am immediately attacked by two 90 lb. slobbering dogs who jump on me, rip my skin, and drool all over my newly cleaned and pressed trousers. The owners of these beasts always laugh, oblivious to my plight. I hear, "they are excited, because they are happy to see you!" I say, "for Chrissakes, every time I come here, it's the same thing!" "Why in the hell can't you put them in the basement, or in your football-field-sized, fenced in backyard?!!!" The pet owners say, "Oh, they're just a little bit rambunctious today; Why don't you lighten up?" During the time this exchange is taking place, my wife is either kicking one of my legs or jabbing me in my ribs.

These pet lovers actually spent big money to send the two mongrels, to doggie obedience school. Apparently, the animals are retarded, because they didn't learn too much about obedience. I know my wife hates my behavior when I visit, but I refuse to be mauled and carried off like road kill.

Cats are not much better. However, I do respect their "fuck you" attitude, and aloofness. Cats seem to be more dignified and mysterious, so I favor them over dogs. The cutesy charm of kitty-cats ends, when one of these hairy creatures chooses to sit in my lap. It always ends up digging its' claws in my thigh, totally content to use my $90 slacks for a scratching post. Since I have pretty quick reactions, I usually can grab the feline by its collar and loft it across the room, up against a wall. The little bells on the collar ring when contact is made. The utterances coming from the little pussy cat, sound like a demon's wail, from a cheap grade-B horror flick. My brutality is followed by sheer shock and horror, of all the people in the room who have witnessed my heinous crime. I profusely apologize, and explain about the pain inflicted on me by the demon cat. Naturally, I am to blame, and the poor kitty is stroked and protected from further aggression. Everyone looks at me with daggers in their eyes. I am now a social outcast. I am an animal abuser! The rest of my afternoon is one of compliance, and profuse apologies.

Thankfully, the feline is significantly more intelligent than the slobbering dogs, and hides for the rest of our visit. I ask for an antiseptic and band aids for my wounds, but I get neither. I feel the icy cold stares coming from all the cat lovers, and my wife. I've learned not to try and legitimize my violent response. This action just creates greater dissonance. I sit there humbled, and wheeze for the rest of the afternoon. The cats' hair is all over me, and its' dander is making my eyes tear. I beg my wife to cut the visit short, so I can go home, attend to my wounds, and take some allergy medicine. I fear the tongue lashing I am going to receive from her on the way home. In a previous chapter, I told you how cats develop neurosis. They all start out like little angels, peeing and pooping nicely in their litter box.

All a responsible owner has to do is to make sure the litter is clean for them every day. We had a couple of cats, and it was my job to scoop clumps of urine and feces from the box every morning. (Try this with a hangover!) I held my breath as

I worked at this chore. I made sure that I double-bagged the nasty stuff in plastic bags from the grocery store. I then placed them in a larger, air-tight container in the garage, till garbage pick-up-day. In hot weather, imagine what joy I had emptying that receptacle. I also had the job of washing out the litter box, a couple of times a week! (We do it all for love.)

When cats go bad, they start spraying everywhere. It's bad enough they're 'ralphing' up hair balls all the time. Once they start peeing in my new golf shoes, or against the new Italian marble wall, in the recently remodeled bathroom, (which cost me twenty-grand), it's time to pack them in their veterinary cages, and bring them to the animal shelter! I try not to look at them, but I hear them crying in fear. They know what I am about to do. I feel like Judas Iscariot. Even though my wife says I did the right thing, I realize in my heart-of hearts that she thinks of me as an insensitive murderer. These kitties were her babies. I just signed the termination papers. I have to live with this, for the rest of your life.

It amazes me how much money we spend on our pets. People buy animal toys, beds, clothing, vitamins, food, treats, veterinary care, shots, collars, leashes, and boarding for them, when they can't bring their little darlings on vacation. Some people are so insane that they dress up ceramic geese, which sit on their front porches.

What astounds me the most, is that some of the same people can ignore the mentally ill, or down-on-their-luck, homeless people. These people are dirty and begging in the streets. These people are human beings! We usually see them on expressway ramps, or sleeping in alleys. Some of these dirty people are veterans of foreign wars, who stood up and defended this country when their names were called. We don't like to look at them. We sure don't want them in "our" neighborhood.

They ought to get a job. We keep sending our money to Bangladesh, Darfur or the Sudan. How about here? If we gave half the money to deserving homeless people, that we spend on our cats and dogs, or send overseas, maybe we could make a difference. Maybe some poor American could clean up, and get a job, or at the very least get a hot meal and a place to sleep. After all, we Americans would never leave an animal out in the freezing cold. It would be too inhumane.

***

WHEELCHAIR ATHLETES

I used to see them when I was young, and ran marathon races. We all went the 26.2 mile distance. The race officials started out the wheelchair athletes first. Talk about hardcore dedicated athletes, these wheelchair competitors showed as much heart as most world class runners.

Imagine how many times two arms, and calloused hands have to turn the wheels of a wheel chair to finish the 26.2 mile race. They all wore gloves, but their hands still were bloodied and blistered, by the end of the race. Their torsos bend with each stroke. Their backs, and abdominal muscles really have to work hard. Wheelchair athletes are rugged competitors. They also have to be smart. They design chairs suited to their specific needs. The chairs have light alloy wheels, and a variety of custom components which give the athlete more speed and dexterity. There are many sports for them to compete in. Marathon racing isn't the only game in town. They play basketball, football, and a game which they fondly call, "Murder ball". The murder ball game is actually wheelchair rugby. These athletes have their own Olympic competition. These guys are the best in the world. One chair can hit an opposing players chair broadside, and dump its' occupant out on the floor, bloodied and in great pain. I've watched these guys play. They are some of the toughest men, I have watched compete in any sport. These guys drink awesome amounts of beer, before and after their victories. Most of them have good looking girl friends or wives.

They sure don't let their disabilities slow them down in the game of life! They don't see themselves as victims. They joke around with one another, laughing at their disabilities. These are men and women who make it all work in their lives. They defy the odds, and come out as winners. They never ask for any special favors. All they expect from 'normal' people is for them to view people with disabilities, as equals, no more, no less. They aren't too much different than you or me. They just happen to lack the use of their legs and sometimes arm or hand development or flexibility. These people were dealt a bad hand, but made themselves champions, through their guts and determination. Everyone of them who competes at whatever level, is an inspiration to me.

So, if you ever want to feel sorry for yourself...Or want to whine about how things are going wrong in you life, think about the wheelchair athletes. I often tell my wife, if I ever lose my legs because of my peripheral artery disease, I wont be sad for too long a time. There are marathons out there for me to compete in. I will practice to roll one with my heroes. In life, people who want to maintain good vibrations, always have a plan "B".

***

THE GAS STATION ATTENDANT

His name was Ernest Voss. He lived in Effingham, Illinois. He was of German stock, thick and strong, but "dumb as a box of rocks". The children at the local school made fun of him. He was slow in his classes. His mother and father were strict Lutherans. Their small house was humble, but clean. Ernest had a brother and two sisters. The brother went to work in the coal strip mines with his Dad. The daughters got pregnant in their teens, and ran off with their spouses of choice. One husband worked at the local grocery store, the other worked on a small farm.

Ernest's dad wanted him to mine coal. The men in the family always worked the mines, going back four generations, when Great Grandpa Voss came over on the boat. He came through Ellis Island with his wife and child, but failed to make his mark in New York. He made his way via the Illinois Central Railroad, to Southern Illinois. He was just nineteen years old with a wife, a two year old, and another one on the way. Great Grandpa was big and strong. The mines ate him up right away. He died of consumption at the age of forty. He lay in a cemetery in back of the house, where all the Voss family members would someday finally rest.

The so-called school psychologists labeled Ernest as a 'dull-normal', after they gave him a battery of psychological tests. His intelligence quotient ranged between 80 and 90 points. The mining company gave him a chance anyway, because his father and brother were good workers, but he just wasn't quick enough on the uptake. He was discharged after a couple of weeks.

Ernest found a job at a gas station outside of town. He rode an old Schwinn bicycle to work every day. Mentally, he had a fourth grade education. He started there in 1956, when he was 16 years old. His mom packed a lunch for him every day. Ernest loved the gas station job right from the start. He was proficient at cleaning the windshields, filling tires with air, checking the oil, and pumping gas. He always was courteous to the customers, and had a big smile on his face all the time. People liked his easy going ways. He studied road maps and enjoyed directing strangers, usually from Chicago, to their various destinations.

The owner of the gas station loved Ernest as if he were his own son. He and his wife never had children of their own. He taught Ernest how to replace spark plugs, and to change air filters and oil. Ernest learned slowly, but wouldn't give up. The reading came hard to him, but with practice and miles of patience from the gas station owner, Ernest learned how to be a good mechanic. Pretty soon, he was pulling engines, and doing brake jobs. Ernest missed pumping the gas, but the owner needed an 'extra set of hands' in the garage. By 1958, Ernest had his own car...a beautiful 1949 Mercury Sedan. Ernest turned this car into a gem of an automobile. Pretty soon, he was out dating girls. He didn't drink or smoke and listened to his mom and dad. He was a spiritual man, who believed in God and family. Women liked him, because he was soft spoken and handsome. He found a pretty girl, with whom he fell in love with, and they married in the little Lutheran Church in town.

Business was flourishing, and Ernest became the shop manager. The owner built a bigger garage, and had 3 mechanics and 2 gas pump attendants working for him now. He also employed an elderly woman behind the counter to sell cigarettes, coffee, and work gloves. She also did the credit card transactions. Ernest was now making more money than his father and brother combined. They were proud of him. Ernest built a big house for his wife and himself when the first baby was on the way. All the family members marveled at how beautiful the structure was. Ernest also became a self-taught carpenter, without ever reading a blue print. He planted flowers, and put up a pretty white picket fence. He also built a nice garage for his tools and car.

Ernest always worked hard, but his family was always his real joy. He was always available for his elderly mom and dad, when they couldn't do the chores anymore. He was always there for his brother, sisters, wife, and children. The owner of the gas station was getting on in years and in 1977, asked Ernest if he wanted to buy the gas station. He offered Ernest a fair price, so he accepted the deal. The town bank gave Ernest the money without question, because he had a fine reputation in the community. He also had a tidy savings account, and had made good on his home loans.

Ernest worked 6 days a week for many years. He put his three children through college. One became a pharmacist, the other a dietician, and the last one a stockbroker in a big firm, way up in Chicago. Ernest belonged to the local Jaycees, the Lutheran Men's Club, and was an organizer for many of the towns civic events. At night he liked sitting on the porch with his wife, hugging her and gazing at the stars. He liked to take her fishing on the lakes in the Shawnee National Forest. Their love for each other, grew stronger and stronger over the years.

One day, his youngest son called him up and said, "Dad, for goodness sakes', You're 70 years old, and you've never been up here in Chicago!" "When are you going to get out of the woods, and explore the world?" Ernest answered his son by saying, "Why would I want to go up there, when God gave me everything I could ever want, right here, in beautiful Effingham, Illinois!" The son just smiled. He knew better than to argue with his dad. Ernest said, "When you gonna' bring my grandbabies down here, so we can go fishing?" That "dumb box of rocks" named Ernest, had gotten pretty darned smart over the years!

***

JOY

Joy is waking up at seven in the morning...
For 33 years my wake-up time was five.
Joy is leisurely reading the morning newspaper...
not having to rush...looking at the chipmunks in my
backyard.
I sip and really taste my coffee...this is joy.
Joy is not having to run a bulldozer anymore,
Outside, in the oppressive heat or cold.
I feel for my union brothers, and know their pain.
Joy is still being healthy enough to go to the gym and
work out,
so that my mind and body are strong. Two hours a day
gives me relaxation,
and clarity of thought,
for the rest of my day.
Joy is painting, writing, or visiting friends.
Joy is dining out, and having an extra piece of pie.
Joy is being sober for five years,
and not having to smoke cigarettes anymore.
Joy is living in an age where modern medicine, and
dedicated physicians and nurses,
work long hours to keep me alive, and functional.
Joy is seeing my daughter grow up into a fine young
woman.

Joy is seeing her love an honorable young man, who will soon be my son-in-law.

Joy is being in love with my wife, and knowing she still loves me, after all these years.

There are so many things to be thankful for in life. I just have to take the time to look for them. Material things are nice, but do not produce real joy. Two weeks before my brother died, in December of 2007, he told me something I will never forget. He said, "I'm looking out my window at my new Lincoln, and at all the possessions in my beautiful home." "They don't mean anything to me anymore, because they are just things." My brother Jim, was acquiring wisdom while facing his own mortality.

Joy is holding a baby's hand. Joy is sitting out on the front porch while watching and smelling the rain. Joy is holding a flower or catching lightning bugs. You make the choice every day. Do I want to be happy or miserable? We all have this power. From the poorest of the poor to the richest of the rich... the simple decision to choose joy over pain and misery, defines each and every one of us.

***

HEARING AIDS AND WATER PICS

I hate wearing hearing aids. I have these state-of-the-art, digital hearing aids. I never wear them anymore. You can't wear a hat with them because the feedback noises are intolerable. The hearing aids can't be worn in the rain, or at the gym. The batteries always decide to die, when I need them the most. I always forget to carry the spares. I have to fiddle around with them constantly to adjust the volume for each situation I encounter. At night they have to be dismantled and cleaned, or else they plug up with ear wax. Who the hell wants to do this much work?...Not me, baby!

It's a lot easier for me, being deaf. I just nod my head and smile all the time. This works for me. Nobody cares what I think anyway, and they are happy that I agree with them, because I am smiling. This simple gesture always works for me! I bring my wife with me to important events to whisper, or rather scream, important information in my ears, to let me know what another individual wants me to understand. I just pretend I am in Japan, and that she is my interpreter. I need her sometimes to help me sell my books or paintings, at book signings and art openings.

Another benefit of being deaf, is not being able to hear the terrible things people say about me. I just keep smiling, nodding my head in affirmation. What a joy! This must really piss my enemies off! It's fun to pretend you don't hear certain instructions, when you'd rather be doing other things. My wife will say, "Didn't you hear that I wanted you to pick up my dry cleaning today?" I say, "No dear, I must not have heard you." It's as simple as that; I'm off the hook! As you can see, deafness certainly has it's advantages. These salient qualities I have elucidated about deafness, might come in handy for you someday!

Another thing I hate to do, is to brush my teeth, and floss after each and every meal. I have to floss and water-pic the hell out of myself, because I am a geezer, and have advanced periodontal disease. I must attend to this grave matter! I want to keep most of my teeth, until they put my ashes in the psychedelic urn. Plastic 'choppers' have to be a bummer. You don't taste your food with these devices, and you have to clean the yucky day old food out of them.

Another problem I have, is with the blood thinners I take for my cell coagulation levels. They make my gums bleed if I get too over-aggressive with my water pic. I can visualize the headlines right now: "Man bleeds to death in bed." "Wife sues Barr Pharmaceuticals, Walgreen's, and the manufacturing company of Water-Pic." My sweet wife is going to make out! God bless America! If I need any dental work done, I have to nix the blood thinners for a couple of days and take penicillin so my oral bacteria won't compromise the Gortex bypasses I have in my femoral arteries. Being off the blood thinners for a couple of days, freaks me out! What if I die from a pulmonary embolism? At least my teeth will be clean and shiny, and Debbie will make sure I am wearing clean underwear before the ambulance comes to take me to intensive care. It's sure hard work getting older!

***

THE NOT SO WILD LIFE

I want to throw on a tank top with skulls and crossbones, and pull on my favorite worn-out Levi jeans. I want to slip on my fancy cowboy boots. I add Navajo jewelry, rings, bracelets, and a cool, silver Indian necklace, to grace my bull neck. I want to pack just the essentials I will need in a beat up back pack for the road trip. I'll jump on that big Harley, and head out west in June for South Dakota, and then on to New Mexico.

I don't want to ride with anyone. I want to do it alone. I want to park my bike along the Rio-Grande, south of Taos, and north of Santa Fe. I will gaze into those river waters. I will look at that blue sky and the snow capped mountains once again. I want to buy jewelry from the Navajo and Pueblo in Santa Fe. I won't buy from the shop owners. The Indians deserve the sales, and are more honest in pricing their jewelry.

I will visit the art galleries on Canyon Road, and walk the two or three miles trying to peddle my paintings to the wealthy, from my beat up portfolio. I will bed down, crashing with the hippie-biker types I make friends with along the way. I pay them back by buying them cheap wine and groceries. We listen to the music of our past. I listen to their tall tales as they smoke reefer and drink cheap whiskey. I bunk down sober, thanking them for their hospitality.

The next morning I treat them to a Mexican breakfast, resplendent with eggs, hot cheese, toast, chorizo sausage, sweet hot coffee, and orange juice. We hug, kiss, and say goodbye. We exchange web sites, business cards, and vow to meet up again.

I do a service check on my Road King. I adjust my brakes, lash down my bags, and tighten down any loose nuts with my wrenches. I check my tires, and gas up for the ride through Albuquerque, down to Las Cruces. I don't dig Albuquerque too much, so I don't stop. The trip down to Las Cruces is windy and hot. I love it that way. This place is mystical for me. It's a land of scrub brush, cactus, rock formations, and rattlesnakes. The bars in town serve great steaks and sandwiches. I like rock climbing, exploring, and praying to the Great Spirit on the outskirts of Las Cruces. The desert puts me in the arms of God. I stay there for three days and head North to Albuquerque, then East through Texas, Oklahoma, and Arkansas. I finally hit Interstate Highway 57, and head north to the magic of Southern Illinois. I take old highway 51 through Anna, Illinois. Now I am seeing places from my past.

I smile as I'm motoring on my big hog. The previous evening, I was bunking with an old Indian friend of mine in Oklahoma. We ran bulldozers together building roads in Illinois, eighteen years ago. He still has a youthful smile and muscled body. The drink didn't get him, thank God, but we both notice the age we have on us now. We laugh and tell stories. We pray together. I hug him as I leave, and give him some magical colored stones I found in the New Mexican desert.

I stop my dreaming, because I'm approaching the house of my Professor friend who I will bunk with, south of Southern Illinois University. While he is teaching, I go hiking and fishing in the Shawnee National Forest. For three evenings, my Professor friend and I discuss art, philosophy, and politics. The visit is enlightening and long overdue. We say our goodbyes, and I head back up Interstate 57 for Wheaton, Illinois. I look dusty, and stink of sweat, just like the raggedy vagabond I am.

I pull into my suburban driveway, gunning that big old motorcycle. The throaty rumble of the Harley is unmistakable to those initiated in the ways of our subculture. I suppose I look anachronistic in my suburban driveway. My neighbors don't stare at me. Instead, they take quick furtive looks, pretending not to see me. I see them whispering to each other. I imagine they are saying, "The madman artist is back, from Lord only knows where." They might continue, "Imagine what it must look like in his house!" I dismiss my negative thoughts immediately, because they are bad for my Karma.

I like looking like an outsider. I'm really a pussycat inside of my heart. My Dharma is to bring joy to all, who are receptive to it. I must tend to the rose garden in my heart and mind. I take a hot shower for a very long time. I fix myself a green tea. I meditate for twenty minutes. Then I think, "The Great Spirit has given me this wonderful day."

***

THE THREE DOLLAR MOVIE SHOW

For three bucks, a person can still see a current full length feature film, on the big screen. There are reasons however, that the movie show comes so cheap! The seats in the show are dilapidated, and caved-in, from 300 lb. popcorn eaters who have been sitting in them for the last thirty years. The floors in this type of theatre are rarely mopped. Your shoes stick to the floors, like a fly sticks to fly paper. Women bring their screaming brats to these cheapie shows. There are a lot of people with NASCAR t-shirts, and missing teeth sitting right in front of you. They always talk during the movie, and usually smell like whiskey. The screen has a hole in it the size of a tennis ball, which distracts me every time I am there. Our feature film always seems to be shown in the #4 viewing room, where the holey screen exists. The movie reels are beat up by the time they get to these cheap shows. The kids at the concession stands always burn the popcorn, and I have to fight for breath, due to the smoke from burning oil, which attacks my emphysemic lungs. The air-conditioning is set real high, so that the movie show owner saves money on his electric bill. Usually, I am hot and sweaty when I leave the cheapie movie house.

My wife Debbie loves these theatres. I can't figure it out. I hate crowds and waiting in line. I'd rather rent two movies for two bucks, order a pizza, and stay in the comfort of my own home. I can always pause the movie, when I need to 'tinkle' in my bathroom. Plus, I don't have to worry about anyone smashing into my new sedan in the parking lot. At home, I can fart and burp at will, and take my socks off. I can't scratch my balls and sit in my underwear at the movie show. For me, the best way to view a movie is in total comfort. I'm trying to convince my wife to allow me to purchase a nice 60" flat screen TV with all the bells and whistles. I can add a nice surround sound system to it. I'd like the sounds to pulsate through my body with such force, that they make a heart pacemaker go totally dysfunctional. Now, that's a total movie experience! I can buy 3 remote controls I don't understand, Tivo, 969 channels I don't use, extra movie channels, pornography stations, games, and every single sporting event known to man, which shows and re-shows, 24 hours a day, 7 days a week! As long as I can order carry-out food, I never have to leave my den ever again, except to go work out at the gym, or to the Funeral Home, if somebody I know happens to die, and screw up my viewing schedules. Just think of the gas money I will save! When I ramble on like this, my wife looks at me incredulously and walks away, shaking her head in disgust. She doesn't get it. Women are certainly strange creatures. Oh well, pass the popcorn.

***

VIKINGS

I wish I was born a Viking. My ancestors came from Denmark. Danish men are all squat and muscular. Most of us are pretty big boys who have pink, ruddy faces. My wife calls me 'Pinky' because of my complexion, but don't tell anyone I told you so! Her pet name for me kind of unfortunately stuck, to the seemingly endless amusement of my so-called, 'friends and family'. My dad had a more masculine nickname. All his friends called him 'Swede'. This moniker never made any sense to me, since my dad was Danish; but Swede sounds a lot more masculine, than Pinky.

Anyway, Vikings were imposing figures. I loved their outfits. They wore big, pointed helmets, with horns coming out of the sides. They had long tangled hair, and big, bushy, red beards. All of them had huge arms hanging out of these keen looking leather vests, which were topped off with metal breast plates. The armor was decorated with threatening looking icons like skulls, dragons, and all kinds of neato stuff like that! They wore loose, baggy pants that looked like burlap. They had big old boots that were lashed together tightly with suede, criss-crossed fashionably all the way up to their knees. They also had awesome looking shields, big-assed swords, head-pounding hammers, giant two-sided hatchets, and leather gauntlets on their huge wrists which went all the way up their forearms!

The Vikings were beautiful in all their menacing glory. They waged war, raped, murdered, and plundered at will all over Europe. They were bad 'Mofo's' man! They controlled the seas as well, with their beautiful Viking ships. The Vikings knew how to party with the best of them! They had lodge parties where they drank alcoholic beverages out of huge pewter tankards which they held in one hand; while the other hand held a big old leg of mutton, or wild boar. The big men slobbered down the meat and mead, while the juices dripped down their raggedy beards. Then they slammed their empty tankards down on the big oak tables, and wiped the meat and suds off their mouths with the sleeves of their jackets. They were really awesome! I never went to a fraternity party in college that ever topped a Viking fling!

In all the movies I've seen about the Vikings, gorgeous, long-haired, blonde barmaids are constantly refilling the Viking's mugs with giant pitchers of brew. All the Viking waitresses had humongous breasts spilling out of their dresses. The Viking guys always grabbed a wench whenever they pleased. They pulled the maidens onto their laps, and dug underneath the women's skirts with their greasy hands. (They never had to tip them, like in the Lap-dance bars!) They'd kiss the girls on their mouths, play grab ass at will, then drag them off to the haylofts to have their way with them! All the wenches laughed and enjoyed the gay ribaldry! No Viking warrior was ever rejected by the comely females. The Vikings were gods in their lodge houses, and demanded to be treated with respect and admiration!

These men often fought and wrestled amongst themselves for the pure pleasure of the violence. Manliness was the credo they lived by, and died by. The Vikings who were lucky enough to live to an old age, were revered and respected by the community. Most of these men died young in battle, or succumbed to a variety of diseases.

When an elder died, he received a Viking funeral. His cohorts wrapped his body in his finest clothing and armor. His sword and shield were placed next to his body. They then placed him in a beautifully decorated, sea-worthy vessel. He was laid out in style, with his favorite possessions surrounding him. I'm sure the old pewter tankard, which held many a round of mead, was included. The dead Viking's dog was murdered, and laid at his feet, to keep him company in the afterlife. Then the ship was set ablaze and cut loose from the mooring. Prayers for the safe journey of his soul were said by his fellow combatants, as the ship sailed off into eternity, in a blaze of glory.

A huge party celebrated the death of a great warrior. Eating, drinking, fornicating, and violent acts were enjoyed by all. This all sounds like a wonderful life for a man! There was no need for therapy, rehab, colonoscopies, or political correctness. If you didn't like someone, or something they said, you ran him through with your trusty sword, or whacked him on the head with your hammer. Things were settled quickly and decisively by the good-old Vikings. Back in the eighth to tenth centuries, they ruled the world. I think their life-style inspired the old adage: "Live hard, die young, and bury a good looking corpse." The Vikings sure didn't spend their old age wringing their hands in doctor's waiting rooms, or laying in hospital beds, trying to fight the inevitable. Maybe they died young, but damn it, they had some good times! They went out like men. Yes, I wish I had been a Viking!

***

THE ZEN OF GROCERY SHOPPING

Grocery shopping sucks! First, I have to frantically hunt for a coveted parking space. Everything is taken, especially on a Saturday or a Sunday. I'd shop at midnight, but I like sandwich meats, and the deli counter is shut down at this particular time. People are always in a big rush. I shop slowly, just like a turtle. I peruse the unit prices and make educated choices, so I usually get more for my money. I always make sure to park my shopping cart out of the way, so people can get past me. I hate people who disregard this basic, unwritten rule. I patiently stand in front of the offenders, staring blankly at them as if I'm in a trance. Eventually, they finally get the clue that I need to pass. I never get angry. Sometimes I look at my watch to time how long it takes them to realize what they are doing to the flow of traffic. The longest I have had to wait is three minutes. Wow! This time needs to be listed in the Guinness Book of World Records! This particular blockage created a great traffic jam of shopping carts behind me. People were shouting at me to assert myself, and tell the offending road hogs to get out of the way. I didn't say a word. I was greatly amused by the whole psychodrama of the event. I pointed at my ears and mouth, and pretended I was a deaf-mute. This messaging system blew their minds! I like being a bad boy. Heeee!

Today my chocolate covered raisins were sold out. I had to settle for Reese's peanut butter cups. It was no big deal.

At about the same time, the liquor department lady came on the store microphone, to announce she was giving away free shots of flavored vodkas. God help me. This is not the kind of information a recovering alcoholic needs to hear, especially after he discovers his chocolate covered raisins are unavailable. I say the Serenity Prayer and decide to stay sober.

Every Sunday, I purchase a cheap ninety-nine-cent get well card for my cousin Ginger. She has the same type of brain tumor as Senator Ted Kennedy. Every week I write her a letter, and send the card out to her on Monday morning. This gives my grocery shopping purpose, and keeps a smile on my face.

My wife Debbie and I have a routine in the store. We know where we are going, and where the other spouse will be at any given moment. We have it down to a science. I always make sure the bagger puts my heavy water bottles, and exercise drinks up on top of the cart. I hate wrenching my back, trying to fish these heavy containers from the bottom shelf of the cart.

I really hate people jamming their carts in the backs of my ankles when I am standing in line. If I am in a really festive mood, I double up in pain and lay down on the floor. I show the perpetrator of this heinous crime, the horrible scars I have on my legs, from my bypass surgeries. I totally freak them out! Debbie just walks away from me, when I do this. I have trouble suppressing my laughter and glee when I am such a bad boy, but my acting job is always worth the effort! Hopefully, I teach these rude individuals a lesson in common courtesy.

Lately, I've noticed that fresh fruit isn't as sweet as it used to be. It must be the chemicals the farmers are using. Sometimes meat from the Deli turns rancid really quickly. Maybe this phenomena is more noticeable to me, because I'm sober and can taste and smell my food. When I drank a half-a-fifth of scotch every day, and smoked a couple-of-packs of cigarettes, a meal of shoe leather with mustard on a Kaiser roll, tasted just fine to me! This was one of the few advantages of being an alcoholic. Anything tasted good to me, if I was loaded! I buy a lot of fresh food now that I am retired. I stay away from all the processed stuff like frozen pizzas, and all the packaged crap with the chemicals in it. I don't buy ice cream, potato chips, or junk foods. My main vice is the darned chocolate covered raisins. Every day, after I drive my sweetheart to work, I go to the gym and work out for a couple of hours. When I get home I hang up my sweaty clothes to dry, and hit the shower. I put on my fresh clothes and check my emails. When I come upstairs from my office, it's usually around one or two in the afternoon. I am ravenous. I make a gut busting sandwich, hot veggies, three or four exchanges of fresh fruit, and a power bar for desert. I set the phone on the end table next to me and watch a "cheapo" movie, chosen from my cable TV menu.

I never make it to the end of the movie. I catch myself snoring at about 2:30 p.m. Grocery shopping makes these wonderful, afternoon siesta moments possible in my life. I try to keep these lovely memories fresh in my mind every Sunday, while I meander my way through the insanity of the people in the aisles. If I can keep my mind focused on the ultimate goals, and the attending joys which come from my efforts, my grocery shopping experience can be wonderfully liberating! Even after listening to the logic of my grocery shopping philosophies, my wife still contends that I have lost my mind. Maybe she's right, but who cares? I'd rather be a happy madman, than a rational or miserable, shopping grinch!

***

PARTYING WITH MENSANS

People who belong to the Mensa Society are a strange group of 'ducks'. These special individuals are the smartest 2% of people in the whole wide world! To be a Mensan, a guy or gal has to take a rigorous intelligence test. My wife says the test proved to be, a couple of hours of sheer mental torture! An attorney friend of ours, who was a Mensan, convinced my wife Debbie to take the test. He overlooked the possibility of me ever having a chance at passing. I just figured he was an elitist, and never appreciated my special talents, so to hell with him! Anyway, to my undeniable amazement, she passed! My Gawd! I always considered her a bright girl, but I never suspected that she was this smart! Once she became a member, Deb started dragging me along with her to club meetings at the Sheraton Hotel, up in Arlington Heights, Illinois. We went to hear lectures, and eat lousy hors-d'ouevres in a couple of small conference rooms reserved by the Mensa Society.

The lectures were fascinating. I listened to hour long treatises, on the mating of Tsetse flies in Africa, the making of beer by Incas in Peru in medieval days, Global warming horror story statistics, and tales of alien sightings and takeovers in obscure places in New Mexico. They also covered the governmental cover-ups of these alien events. All of this stuff was great fun, except due to my alcoholism, I couldn't imbibe in the great varieties of foreign bottled beers, served at every meeting.

Many of the members were either physically or mentally impaired in one way or another. I saw a lot of people with thick glasses, hearing aids, and walking devices. Some were afflicted with strange forms of neurosis, which caused them to twitch uncontrollably, or shout out obscenities. These genius types walked into doorways and fell down once in a while. In essence, "they couldn't walk, and chew gum at the same time." Being the insensitive buffoon that I am, I always went wild with laughter at the expense of these physically, or mentally challenged geniuses. My wife was stern with me, elbowing me in the ribs, or giving me 'the look' whenever I got out of line. On occasions when I raised my hand after a lecture, to ask what I thought was an extremely intelligent question, my wife hurriedly pulled my arm down. I had a tons of fun!

Mensan's are game freaks. One whole room was devoted to various board games and the like. Mental gymnastics ruled on Saturday nights! Can you imagine wasting your time doing brain busters on a Saturday night? What's worse, was the fact that a lot of these geeks were young people! When I was young on a Saturday night, I drank shots and beers in my favorite watering holes. I danced with leggy females. I gambled on pool tables and listened to rock and roll. I guess I wasn't very smart, but hell, I sure had some good old times! After a while, even Debbie tired of Mensa. I told yah' my wife was a bright girl!

***

WHAT MY GUT TELLS ME

I think it might be time to sell my suburban town home, cash in all my chips, so to speak, and buy some acreage up in Northern Montana or Wyoming. I need a place somewhere desolate, where nobody wants to live. My gut tells me we are about to implode here, in the "good old U.S.A". I smell fear and anger. It's going to get damned bloody, before we hit bottom.

Twenty acres of land will do, for me and my family. I need to buy a beat up D-5 Caterpillar Bulldozer. I'll need a wide-track model, which has excellent flotation in the mud. I'll buy an old 955 track end loader as well. I'll need to buy cable, dynamite, fence post, barbed wire, and chain link fence material. I'll have to build myself a hydraulic log-splitter as well. I will cut out the root balls from all the trees with the dozer blade and knock em' down with the end loader. I'll have to send a lot of the good logs to the mill, so they can be planed for my new cabin. The dozer and loader will help me build my entrance road, and the building pads for my cabin and pole barn. My land will be fenced in with barbed wire, and no trespassing signs will be posted at 20 ft. intervals. The fence will have to be electrified, and I'll need to buy and train four or five mean Dobermans to patrol the property. I don't trust pit-bulls. They can turn on a man.

I'm going to need some weapons as well. I'm thinking about purchasing a couple of Uzi's, an M-16, and maybe a couple of Glock clip-type automatic hand guns. I already have a lot of outerwear for the cold, but need to stock up on rough canvas, Carhart coveralls, wool socks, boots, etc. I'll need to buy kerosene lanterns and salamanders. Also I'm going to have to purchase a big old pot belly stove. I'll have to build a pole barn for my tools and farming implements. Then there's the task of building a barn for my livestock and horses. I'm going to need feed, seed, fertilizer, chickens, hogs, and chicken coops. I'm also going to need mason jars, non-spoilable food items, augers, and furrowing attachments for my tractor. I have enough money to buy all this stuff for cash. My back and the backs of the chosen few men and women who decide to pitch in with me, are going to do the bullwork to build this encampment. Hopefully, they will purchase land which abuts mine. I'd like to get 4 or 5 families involved in this project. There is safety in numbers. I need some young families who have vision and are committed to this kind of lifestyle. I'll need them because there are some things my older body cannot do anymore...but if I have to do it all myself, I will find a way, or die trying.

Energy dynamics will include solar panels, geo-thermal energy, rain catchers, windmills, septic tanks, and underground housing, to save on the costs of heating systems and air-conditioning. I'll need a big old water tower and a couple of underground fuel tanks, like the gas stations have. I will hunt and fish for game. I'll grow vegetables and fresh fruit, to the degree this hard environment allows.

It's a short temperate season way up there. I will have to devise a plan for earth moving, building, and clearing land. I'm going to have to negotiate all of this between the months of June and September. Four months is not a lot of time, so I will have to work twelve hours a day, seven days a week, to provide minimum shelter, heat and food, to survive the first winter. A tough, four-wheel-drive vehicle with a winch is a must in this tough country as well. In the not to distant future, I anticipate a migration of like-minded individuals, making the trek up to the northlands to occupy cheap land in these under populated states. I also expect thieves, and neer-do-wells to try to encroach upon my property. My plans take care of these types of miscreants. Heeee!

We are the self-sufficient people who learned to work with our hands and minds. We are the same people who have been over-worked and over-taxed our whole lives. Some call us survivalists. This fact is true, we are going to survive. Hard working people always find a way. If we have to, we will protect ourselves from people who want to steal from us, (if and when economic Armageddon arrives). If it ever comes down to this, I will remember the words of the great Charlton Heston, (supporter of the National Rifle Association). "I will die proudly, holding the cold, blue steel of my weapon, in my cold, dead hands." God bless America! Somehow, a perversion of logic has made me and my kind the renegades in society. So be it!

**

I'M JUST TIRED

Sometimes I just want to give up.
The pain becomes too great for me to bear.
More bad news comes every day.
I find, I have to force myself to pray.
I know I have to carry on.
I must be a man, accept my fate.
I'm just tired, I have to wait, for better news.
Deny the blues.
People depend on me.
Do not fear your destiny.
Be an example of acceptance.
No victim or whiner will I be.
Do it for your family.
But can't they see?...
I'm just tired.
Maybe with these printed words...
My luck will change...It sounds absurd.
For my luck was good...
And now it's time,
To figure out new paradigms.
What makes me think I am immune...
To loss of health, the doom and gloom?
It comes and goes...
These madman's thoughts.

I shouldn't think...I haven't lost.
I'm just tired.

***

GRANDCHILDREN

L ately I think about grandchildren. My daughter won't be married until August of 2009, but my selfish mind wants grandchildren right away! I never thought I'd come to this! I smile and think what an old fool I've become.

A year of college is left for my daughter, and maybe two or three years as an elementary school teacher. Then hopefully, she and her husband Peter will decide to start having babies. Another nine months, and hmmm, let's see, I will be sixty-three or sixty-four. If I make it to seventy-three, which is doubtful, my grandchild will be ten years old. My goal is to stay fit and healthy enough to be able to take the little girl or boy to White Sox games, the Lincoln Park Zoo, movie shows, Ferris wheel rides at Navy Pier, Shedd Aquarium, The Art Institute of Chicago, The Natural History Museum, The Museum of Science and Industry, the top of the Sears Tower, Buckingham Fountain, and Soldier Field to see Bears football games! Whew! I'm getting out of breath. There is so much more to do…I want to tell them about the Chicago I knew as a young man, and what I think about it now, as an old man.

I pretended I was a survivalist yesterday. Today, I'm practicing my future as a grandfather. What strange dream scenarios comprise my mind! Today is a day to give thanks! I am not angry at God today. The thought of grandchildren gives me strength and purpose. Even if Catherine and Peter don't have kids, the dream of my daughter finding a wonderful husband has been fulfilled. My dreams might keep me alive another ten or fifteen years, maybe more! My wife says old curmudgeons like me, who talk about their impending deaths all the time, live long lives. I doubt it!

***

AUTOMOBILE SALESMEN AND DEALERSHIPS

Does anyone in their right mind trust an automobile salesman? I sure don't. I won't even talk to them until I totally research the car I want, its price, and its availability. Where do I search and price? The internet, of course! I look at everything pertaining to the car I want to purchase. Last year, I bought a brand new 2007 Toyota Camry, LE. I think I got a pretty good deal, because I researched the supposed 'bottom line' prices each dealership listed on their websites.

I eliminated many car hawkers. Finally I was content to email three Toyota dealerships. I told them exactly what I wanted in regard to options, model, color, et cetera. I demanded that they NOT contact me by telephone, only by email, or they would negate the possibility of doing business with me. Believe it or not, one of the car dealers contacted me by phone. I said to the young salesmen on the other end of the line, "You know, you just blew a sale'. Didn't you read the email?" "Yes, he said, but my manager wanted me to follow up with a phone call." I told the young man to tell his manager, that I felt he was a bad businessman. He disrespected my request. I would never do business with anyone who didn't respect the wishes of a customer, especially when thousands of dollars were at stake. I am in control of the sale! I hung up on the kid. Now I had only two dealerships to bargain with. Fun time begins!

I never mince words with a car salesman. I tell them to sit and listen to me. I say, "I'm going to buy a new car today, and if you want to make a sale, you are going to get your little pen out of your pocket, and give me your 'rock bottom' price, which includes taxes, license and all applicable fees." This is known as the 'out-the-door' price." I continue my speech, "I also need to know what you are going to give me for my trade-in." "I am shopping at a few other Toyota dealerships today, and if you want to stay in the game, you need to do exactly as I say." "Furthermore, If Toyota doesn't take care of me the way I expect them to, there is always Nissan or Hyundai."

Wow! You should see their jaws drop, after this little prepared speech! Whenever I feel bullshit coming my way, I ask for another salesman. They are there to serve me, not insult my intelligence. Always remember, You control the sale! You have the money and the power, UNTIL you sign on the dotted line! Don't ever let a salesman take control. Get your information, and quickly leave for the next dealership. Then play the same game...Some salesmen want to know how much I'm willing to pay, or who offered me the price on the little piece of paper I show him. (I always drop the 'rock-bottom' price 'a grand' when I show the figure...Heeee!). Never share any information with a salesman...I tell him it's none of his business what I did at another dealership...I tell him, "I'm doing business with you now, forget the other dealership!" Then you play a wonderful game with your cell phone. Watch as their bottom line prices drop lower and lower. When neither of them wont budge anymore, go home and forget about them for a week!

You will receive emails, letters, and phone calls. Act arrogant about the phone calls, during this cooling off period. Squeeze as many extras out of them as you can, like free car washes, oil changes, courtesy rentals, detailing and sealing. Play them like a fine bass fiddle!

Finally, when you think you have a deal, go in and read all the fine print. Look at your new car with a fine toothed comb. Get underneath it, around all its' sides. Open the hood and look at the engine. Make sure everything is perfect! Bring a magnet with you, and make sure the car hasn't been reworked with Bondo. Sometimes they try and sell you what looks like a brand new car, but the vehicle has had body work done. That's why I carry the magnet. Never finance a car if you can pay cash. I buy new cars, because I can afford them. Actually, you are better off buying one a year old, because they still carry warranties, and you can low-ball the price, because the Dealers need to move them off the lot, to make room for the new models.

My greatest joy comes when they smile at me as they shake my hand after the deal is done. I know they are calling me a cheap Polack, or some other expletive in their greedy little minds! They had to sell a car for a lower commission. Never, ever, let a salesman bamboozle you by making you sit for hours. He will try and fake you out by saying he is going in the manager's office, in order to get you a better deal. He and the manager will come out and lie through their teeth. They will tell you it is impossible for you to get a better deal. What they are saying to you is total bullshit! It just makes me sick to think how many people get played like this, by these weasels!

Always try and keep your car for ten years. Never bring it back to the dealership for service. Dealership service departments steal you blind! Get a good ole' boy garage mechanic from Effingham, Illinois to do your maintenance. Some small shops even can do your major engine work for you now, because they send their mechanics to school, and have the computerized engine analysis equipment. Find an honest man who will charge you an honest price. Find a guy who will stand by his work, because he has pride in what he does.

***

THE BODY BUILDER

He came from a middle class home. It sat nestled on a tree lined street, with long driveways, nicely manicured lawns, and flower gardens. His mom and dad drove beautiful, new cars. His dad had a fine job, and made enough money for his mom to devote her entire time as a "stay at home mom". He was an only child and wanted for nothing. He had all the toys a kid could conceivably want. His mom and dad loved him very much and he had a very happy childhood, until he started school.

He didn't like the books. He couldn't grasp the assignments. He made the decision early on in his life that he disliked school. His parents tried remedial schools, tutoring, discipline, and psychologists to get their child on the right track. He was processed into high school, and discovered sports. He was a natural. He excelled at everything. He was a great athlete. He became a star football and baseball player. He also excelled in track and field. All his teachers passed him because of his athletic prowess. The high school looked good, because every team he played on won championships.

While his friends accepted athletic scholarships to various colleges, he turned his down. He still hated school. He worked menial jobs which allowed him to play on semi-pro football teams. He learned that lifting weights, and steroids, was the road to professional football. He was looking forward to signing on a professional team as a free agent, without facing the misery of four years of college. He stood 6 ft. 4 inches tall, and weighed a meager 230 lbs. when he started out. After years of pumping iron, and injecting steroids, he was a solid 280lbs. His body fat composition was an unbelievable 4.5%. He was solid as a rock.

The steroids affected his personality. He had fits of anger. He also developed a severe case of acne, one of the side affects of 'juicing' with steroids. He got into a fight with a couple of guys who were taunting him in some local bar. He broke one man's jaw and another man's ribs. They ended up in the hospital, he ended up in court. When his case finally came to trial, he was given the option of going to jail for two years or enlisting in the Marines…He didn't want to have a felony on his record for assault and battery, so he went the way of the Marines. His parents had to settle, and pay a lump sum to the guys he beat up, per the decision of a judge in civil court. He felt like a failure. So much for his professional football career. He served four years honorably and began winning body building competitions, while still in the service. When he came home, he started training at a local gym, and won every amateur competition in his class. He started making a lot of money from endorsements. By turning pro, and winning more competitions, the money really started rolling in. He was featured in muscle magazines, advertising everything from 'soup to nuts'. He opened up his own gym and nightclub. He drove around in a shiny new Mercedes. He had it made, except he was still using the steroids. He rationalized his drug use by thinking, "Everyone is doing it on the pro-body-building-circuit, and I don't want to lose my edge." He married his childhood sweetheart and they raised three beautiful children. He never cheated on his wife and was a wonderful father.

The only Achilles heel he had, was the 'juicing'. He kept his secret to himself. He thrived on the drug. His muscle high sustained him. He never smoked, and when he drank, it was only a couple of beers, once a week. He took mega-doses of vitamins and protein supplements. He knew more about nutrition than a lot of dieticians and doctors. All was good until he was 50 years old. He started feeling tired all the time. Increasing the steroid dosage wasn't helping his workouts. He looked ashen, and began to drop weight. One day, he collapsed in the gym. They rushed him to the hospital. What he experienced, was a heart attack. All of his organs were oversized and damaged. His cardiologist told him he had major heart damage, 40% of the muscle was gone. His liver enzymes looked terrible. His kidneys were compromised as well. He dropped in weight, down to 200 lbs. When he came back to the gym, he looked like death...a gray ghost...an old man. The road map of veins, muscle definition, and glowing health, had all gone away.

Rumors spread like wildfire in the gym. The news traveled fast. People in the gym started talking about his possible use steroids. His doctors told him he would be signing his own death sentence, if he ever used them again.

About four months later I saw him. He was huge. His face was beet red. His body was enormous with muscle. He pumped enormous amounts of weight, four to six hours a day. He told me, "I need to win just one more National title, then it's all over." "I need this one, then I can retire." I couldn't believe my ears, and how he had gotten so big, so fast. He had to be juicing again. I shook his hand and wished him good luck. I think he was in a state of denial, like a drug addict or alcoholic. I know how I thought when the booze had me in its' grip. I never thought I was doing damage to myself or my family. Steroids or alcohol have a way of fueling narcissism and insanity. It's a sad irony to look so good on the outside, and to be sick and damaged on the inside. We do horrible things to ourselves for fame, fortune, and the acceptance of our peers. Cheap trophies, belts, plaques, prizes, and newspaper clippings aren't worth the beauty of one twenty-four hour day. Choose life and health...Nobody really cares about what you've accomplished in life anyway. Most people are just too busy being self-absorbed.

***

PEOPLE AND THINGS THAT UPSET ME:

1. POLITICIANS: Enough said.
2. CLERGYMEN: Not all, but those who drive Lincolns or Cadillacs, and ask their flock to donate $500 to the church at Christmas time.
3. DIVORCE LAWYERS: These are the guys who meet each other for 3 martini lunches to discuss how long they can keep a legal battle going on between a husband and wife, so they can make more money.
4. ANY RADICAL RELIGIOUS GROUP: More people have been murdered, mutilated, or tortured in the name of God than for any other conceivable reason or cause.
5. AUTOMOBILE SALESMEN: They are right down there, with divorce attorneys. These are two groups of bottom feeders for sure!
6. SOLICITORS: Especially those who call after six in the evening. I'd like to find out who they work for, dial their C.E.O.'s phone number, and try and sell him merchandise he doesn't want—at three-in-the-morning.
7. PEOPLE WHO DON'T GIVE UP THEIR SEATS TO THE ELDERLY.
8. RUDE WOMEN and MEN: Those individuals who drive big SUV's, while putting on makeup, writing things in notebooks, and simultaneously talking on cell phones.

9. LACKADAISICAL HOOKERS: They lie in bed, no smile, deader than mackerels, like lifeless dolls after receiving 5 or 6 Benjamin Franklins for straight sex. (No tips should ever be tendered to these hags!)

10. TREEHUGGERS: Bleeding heart, wealthy liberals who live in 15,000 square foot homes, and spew their vituperative environmental solutions on TV, and then fly all over the country, doing all kinds of damage to the atmosphere due to the pollution streaming from their Lear Jets. These are the types who have Hummers, and gas-eating sports cars sitting in their five car garages.

11. TEASERS: These are the women who wear push-up-bras, short skirts, and spiked heels, who roll their eyes in disgust, or give looks of animosity, when their "merchandise" is happily eyeballed by interested men.

12. DISHONEST CHECK OUT CLERKS: Always count your change!

13. THEIVES: I especially dislike the low-life-types who smash windshields in the wee hours of the morning, in order to grab a purse from some poor old lady who is lost. Little old ladies should always have a .357 Magnum handgun in the glove box, when traveling by themselves. This is why the second amendment should never be questioned by Congress. Harrumph! Use of said weapon can save the taxpayer an enormous amount of money, which is now uselessly spent on housing these criminals.

14. SLOBS: People who throw fast food bags, beer cans, and cigarette butts on the street from moving vehicles.

15. TRAITORS: Anyone who burns or disrespects the American flag, or the American way of life. This category includes dirty politicians, and corporations who send our work to foreign countries for personal gain.

16. IGNORANT PET OWNERS: People who let their dogs shit on my lawn and don't pick up the mess. If I see who does it and know where they live, I box the little turd, douse the box with lighter fluid, put it on their front porch, set it ablaze and ring the doorbell. I hobble across the street quickly, laughing like a teenager and peer through my window as they stomp out the fire! This is great fun for a retired guy!

17. UNRESPONSIVE TELEPHONE AND CABLE COMPANIES: The list of complaints is too long for me to write. I have horror stories that will make your hair curl...I don't want to upset myself, because I wont be able to sleep tonight! Nothing works anymore, and it makes me insane!

18. BRIDEZILLAS: Marriage plans turn cute, little, young women into monsters! Not you Catherine! You're doing a good job! Whew!

19. THE MEDICAL BUSINESS: The whole medical-pharmaceutical, health insurance and welfare machine...The complexity of it all, fear generated by useless tests and surgeries, costs and time spent on the telephone to straighten out problems are mind boggling. I knew I was in trouble when the nurse wrote, "cut here," when I went in for my first leg surgery!

20. ARROGANT AND DANGEROUS CAB DRIVERS: They are abundant in any major city! Watch out for them!

21. ANGRY SERVICE WORKERS: Uncommunicative, sulking bartenders, waitresses, waiters, cashiers, salespeople, barbers, librarians...all people in service type jobs who shouldn't be in them, because they hate people. Their anti-social arrogance is demeaning, and totally unnecessary.

22. TV GUIDE DESIGNERS: A rocket scientist couldn't understand the new TV guide in the Chicago Tribune...It gets worse every week! Why couldn't they leave well enough alone?

23. THE TV SHOW, "THE VIEW": I can't believe what I am hearing. Does this define what has happened to female intelligence, or lack of it in this new culture? Thank God, many good, intelligent women are too busy at work to bother themselves with such banality.

24. REALITY TV SHOWS: This is reality? Thankfully, not in my world!

25. PROFESSIONAL ATHLETES: Whine, whine, whine, whine!...overpaid and mostly uneducated.

26. BULLIES: Both male and female.

27. CRITICS: These professionals make a living from critiquing works of art, literature, film making, food preparation. Most of them never produced anything of merit themselves. If so, what makes them experts?

28. ME: I get carried away all the time. I need to chill out and start painting again! If I didn't put myself on this list, I'd be a total hypocrite!

***

PEOPLE WHO INSPIRE ME

Benjamin Franklin, Albert Einstein, Louis Pasteur, Thomas Edison, Mark Twain, Martin Luther King, Mahatma Gandhi, Mother Theresa, Jane Goodal, Margaret Mead, Will and Ariel Durant, Joseph Campbell, Eckhardt Tolle, Galileo, Fighting Father Flanagan, Mother Cabrini, Franklin Delano and Eleanor Roosevelt, All American Veterans of Foreign Wars, living or dead. All the men and women in the armed forces who protect our country today. Policemen, firemen, social workers, psychiatrists, nurses and doctors, who believe in integrity and compassion. Leonardo DaVinci, Jesus Christ, Muhammad, Buddha, Upton Sinclair, Dr. Bob and Bill W., founders of Alcoholics Anonymous, Jane Adams, the 1985 Chicago Bears Super Bowl team, Walter Payton, Michael Jordan, Steven Spielberg, Martin Scorsese, Clint Eastwood, Sylvester Stallone, Arnold Swarzenegger, William F. Buckley, Steve Allen, George Carlin, R. Buckminster Fuller, Ed Paschke, Colin Powell, Carl Jung, Sigmund Freud, Harry Truman, Jimmy Stewart, Carol Burnett, Bill Gates, Warren Buffet, Gutenberg, George Washington Carver, Muhammed Ali, Paul McCartney, Rosa Parks, John F. Kennedy, Tony Blair, Robert Pirsig, Ralph Ellison, Henry Ford, The Wright Brothers, Studs Terkel, and the workers of the world.

We need our heroes...The list goes on and on for me. It's good to study both sides of the coin. This short list of people gives me hope for the future!

***

MONDAY MIRACLE

I woke up this morning and was surrounded by auras of light. Celestial harp music entered my ears! I floated down the stairs as if on angel's wings. My land line telephone is working. It's a miracle! I pad the way downstairs to my office (while still wearing my underwear), and discover that all the lights are lit on my modem! It's another miracle! I turn on the computer and punch in my AOL password...I am instantly connected! May God, and all the saints be praised! I take back all the evil things I've thought and said about Comcast. I go to the gym and have a fantastic workout. I come home and get on the scale and see that my weight has dropped to 194 lbs.! Miracles continue to come my way.

I check my mailbox and discover to my amazement, that my prescription for Prevacid, (a drug to fight the evil pre-cancerous mucous on my vocal chords, has finally arrived!) The local union hall pharmacy price was only thirty bucks, as opposed to the $196 dollar Walgreen's price. I am on a roll now! I call my old friend Ray, who has been angry with me for the past five years. I make amends to him on the phone. He forgives me and we have a wonderful conversation! Miracles are occurring left and right! I am walking on air! I feel mystical. The sun is shining beautifully now. What started out a bleak, humid, rainy, Monday, has changed into a perfect summer day! Let's keep this magical, Karmic train rolling!

I take my Prevacid, and break my appointment with the service people at Comcast. I call my doctor's nurse, and actually get through to a human voice, in order to schedule my D-Dimer test for my blood coagulation levels. I am ecstatic.

I remember back a few years ago, when the image of the Blessed Virgin Mary inexplicably appeared on the wall of Hubbard's cave, (a busy six lane expressway, underground tunnel, south of Ohio Street in Downtown Chicago.) Devout Mexican, Caucasian, and African American Roman Catholics thought this was a miracle. They placed candles, flowers, crucifixes and other holy items beneath the beautiful icon. The City of Chicago had to shut down a lane of traffic. The rush hour was a mess. Finally the image was washed away either by City workers, rain, or time. I can identify with these religious 'true believers', after having my 'miracle Monday'.

Anything is possible with faith! When a couple of young kids can put a cornflake in the shape of Illinois on Ebay for a thousand bucks, and actually sell it for that price, it's a miracle my friends! I'm going to fix my lunch now, and enjoy my wonderful meal. Afterwards, I will fall asleep in my chair. When I wake up, I'm going to the local convenience store to buy $20 worth of lottery tickets. By tomorrow evening I will be a millionaire! Mark this date on your calendar, July 21st, 2008. This is the day of miracles for me!

I just hope I don't get hit by a car in the convenience store parking lot; or suffer a cerebral hemorrhage by getting too excited about all these wonderful things that have happened to me today. Naw, don't start thinking negative thoughts Richie, baby! You'll jinx yourself. Ride the wave of joy for as long as you can! These miracle days are too few, and far between!

***

CRAZY EDDIE

Chicago Crazy Eddie is 64 years young, and still going strong! He, of Rolling Stones "knock-off-band" fame, Crazy Eddie looks just like Mick Jagger of the Rolling Stones. Eddie has all of Mick's moves, and dances like him as well. Crazy Eddie can still rock and roll! His theme band is appropriately named: "Hot Rocks".

Eddie married his childhood sweetheart Dana. She does most of the bookings, paperwork, and promotional activities for the band. They probably also employ a publicist, and a webmaster. All the guys in the band are up in years. They are aging baby-boomers. They all are family men, still going out to do gigs. Bent but not broken, they still can rock pretty well for themselves. As a young man, Eddie attended the Art Institute of Chicago. He still does "freaky" metal sculptures, in his garage or backyard. He broke a few ribs a few years ago when he laid down his Harley on some dark street in Chicago. Two weeks later, he was singing and hobbling around on stage, in spite of his pain.

Old rockers endure the pain. The show must go on! Eddie and Dana are lovely people, and good friends to my wife and myself. Eddie and Dana come to see me at my art openings whenever they can. They are real Chicago, working class people. They are true-blue, honest, and hard working...They will do anything for you, if you are a friend. They have a grown daughter, who is also an artist. I think the creative gene runs in families. My wife and I continue to see their shows and support the band. God bless you crazy man Eddie...Dana...the band... and your wonderful family! This chapter is for you!

***

JAIL BIRD SUE

She was one of my customers, where I worked pouring shots and beers. It was a biker bar. She owned a lovely smile, and long brown hair. She was walking a tight rope. She lived life on the edge. It was only a matter of time, before she took the fall. DUI's, drug convictions, petty crimes finally got her three months in the Du-Page County Jail. She let us all know the day she had to turn herself in, in order to start serving her time.

She always tipped me well. I liked this girl. She was a fallen angel with a heart of gold. Everyone in the bar promised that they would visit her. As her incarceration date came closer, I saw changes in her demeanor. She grew more tense and agitated. She started drinking a little more heavily. She gained some weight. She knew what she was facing, because she had been there before. I went to see her the first week she was in jail. She put her hand up to the glass, and I put my hand up and pressed it against hers. I didn't feel anything but the cold, wired pane that separated us. The gesture of connecting was enough, though neither one of us felt any warmth. We spoke on the phone. She looked like hell without her heavy eye makeup and lipstick. She looked somewhat disheveled, dark circles under her eyes, redness from crying...

When she smiled at me, it was that same great, broad, sunshine smile. She never gave that up. She had known some joy in her life, but had experienced more than her share of sorrow. I wrote her letters every day. I tried to visit her on rain days, when I couldn't run my bulldozer and had a couple of days off.

I continued to drink and drive, and smoke reefer. I was no better than Sue. "John-Law" just hadn't caught me yet. Sooner or later, the law of averages catches up with people who live our life style. The saddest sound in the world is hearing the jail house door echo, as they lock you in your cell. You are alone in your gloom. You learn jail house customs and mores, and put on your game face. The first dude who messes with you has to pay the price, or else the time you do will be hard. The old saying goes, "If you do the crime, you gotta' do the time."

***

ODE TO SUE

When she got out she shared with me.
Forever thankful, she would be...
I was a true friend, you see.
The only one from the bar to visit her was me...I learned
a lot that day.
Bar room friends will always say..."I'll come and see you
every day."
"I'll come to see you drinkin' buddy..."though the skies
aren't blue, and the parking lot's muddy." You wait and
wait for company...Visiting hours remain empty.
Human nature continues to show its' true face...You
think,
"God damn, I want out of this place."
So here's to you sweet Sue...I don't know what became of
you.
In my heart, I hope you're fine...A nice husband and kids,
to share your time.
A house in the suburbs, a nice green lawn...A life for you,
after the wrong.
I wish you health, wealth, and joy...Cause' I thought, you
were the real McCoy.
A diamond in the rough, you were to me. I could see
through your misery.
You weren't a tough girl. That wasn't meant to be...
Sometimes in life we're thrown together...To share in the
stormy weather.

Your friendship meant something to me...I'm glad I responded, can't you see?

Talk is talk, nothing more...Action is what gets us more...Of the good.

You know now Sue, I'm not a common hood. I kept my word, tried to do you some good, not out of duty, but because I could.

So if this letter finds your hand, be reassured, I'm still the same man...

But better now.

I have matured. This wild life now, I find absurd...

We need to grow Sue, every day...We all must find the simple way.

A moon, a smile, a cloud, a child...

These great treasures keep us from runnin' wild.

***

A SPIDER IN THE CORNER OR MY MIND

There is a spider in the corner of my mind. He waits for me expeditiously. He possesses an economy of movement. Cunning and patient, he is more than a worthy adversary. He is a part of me.

In the corner, he waits for me to lapse into my illogical self. Then, he must work quickly. He knows not when I might snap out of my narcoleptic state to threaten him back into his corner with goodness. He must weave his cocoons of evil quickly. He is rewarded by my evil thoughts. Evil synapses fire, and my brain is rewired for destruction. He is triumphant this time. There are an endless series of engagements in this war. The battles have been going on for a very long time. I am winning more of them now. He won more in the past.

He can destroy a man. He is small but powerful. I must keep my eyes open at all times; I must stay ever vigilant. I take my sleep, but he can enter my dreams and turn them against me. He is EVIL, you see...Yet he remains a part of me.

My spider asks me many questions. He uses his convoluted logic against me. He makes sin appear so luscious, so beautiful! He is convincing, amiable and dangerous. He looks like a beautiful dark red rose, but I must watch out for the thorns. Much in the same way, I must watch out for my spider's subterfuge. The spider lulls me into an anesthetic state and quickly strikes me with his sharp fangs. I feel a warm rush of poison. His venom of evil gets me pleasantly high. I feel omnipotent for a short amount of time, then the hangover and remorse come to me. Then, I know I have lost a battle, a part of my soul. I have lost for a valueless, fleeting moment of pleasure.

I chase him back to his corner with good deeds, prayer, meditation, and determination...but he always comes back. I willingly let him in. Soon, he puts a hairy leg around my shoulder as if he just found a long lost friend. We smile at each other once again. Ours are sardonic smiles...death masks.

They are skull-like smiles celebrating luscious debaucheries. "Have fun," he says, "Life is too short!" "There is nothingness waiting for you...Stay angry...drink again, put a needle in your arm...have a cigarette...fuck that whore...She's gonna' love it when you jam it in her and give it to her hard." "Have a drink...have more than one!...Have the whole bottle!" "Screw the hangover!" "There is no hangover if you have two or three in the morning, asshole!"

This is the spider in the corner of my mind. He goes by many names. He wants me to deny myself, my wife, my child, and all that is good. He wants to wrap up everything that I own, and take it for himself. He wants to weave his evil web and hide all my good qualities in his dark little corner, so that only my evil self remains.

If he owns me, as he has in the past, my whole head becomes his apartment. Then he will own my whole mind. Then he will rule every nook and cranny. Finally, he will emerge victorious! He will rule with fear and keep me tantalized with debauchery. My body will get weaker and ill with each shot of whiskey, with each joint of marijuana, with each lovely cigarette.

My pen will lie still, my paint brushes will dry up from lack of use. My mind will not be my own anymore. It will be in the possession of this black, hairy, entity. My spider is named

Lucifer. He is the arachnid known as pride. He is sin and misery, a Svengali of great mental power. His evil is hypnotic, sensual, sexual, and warming. His evil is always inviting to me. This evil looks hip and contemporary, like a new shiny sports car, and a busty blonde.

The spider says, "Get in your fancy car man!" "Enjoy the ride." "Stick your hand up her skirt, she won't mind." "Offer her a line of cocaine." "Cole Porter was wrong about champagne and cocaine you know!" "You are my brother man, I wouldn't do anything to hurt you!" He is a no-good, lying bastard, this spider of mine. He says to me, "There is no God". "God would not have allowed Auschwitz, Hiroshima, The Inquisition, plagues, droughts and all the other miseries inflicted on mankind, since the beginning of time!" "The church put all the guilt in your feeble mind." "Original sin...Hah!" "You make yourself suffer needlessly, over Apostolic fairy tales." "Wake up and enjoy yourself, you fool!"

I say to him, "All the evils you speak of were caused by you." "The evils that men inflict on each other are caused by self-centeredness, fear, greed, lust, envy, sloth, pride, and gluttony." "You know all of them spider...They nourish you... They are the Seven Deadly Sins!" "There is something good in this universe, which requires men to act with humility and compassion. Men who act within a framework of spirituality for the right purposes, are rewarded with peace of mind." "You cannot justify men acting like animals, ripping at each other mindlessly, to fulfill their perverse desires, whether God exists, or not." "You are the basis of my insanity spider...I refuse to acknowledge you!...So get out of my head!"

These little philosophical conversations, go on day after day, week after week, year after year, between the spider and myself. The chess game continues on the battlefield in my head. I envy people with small spiders or mites. These people are the 'normal ones'. I will do battle with the spider till the day I die. I realize that when I surrender my will and life to the Great Spirit, my fear of the spider goes away. When I am on my guard against evil, and continue to do good works, the spider goes away. At these times, he crawls in the corner of my mind and rolls himself up into a little ball. He knows I am gaining strength over him through my surrender to God's will. In Latin, the word 'surrender' means, to join the winning side. The winning side, is always the side full of good works for mankind. There is no room for hate or fear in God's army. God's strength comes to people at peace. I like the little song, "Let there be peace on earth and let it begin with me."

The spider says, "Oh for Christ's sake, shut up!" "You sound like an elderly Catholic grandmother!" "You're not a man, you're a pussy!...The great men through history waged war, used women, and figured out ways to steal money to better themselves in the eyes of society!" "You're a hypocrite, because you succumb to my evil every day!"

I say, "I'm not a hypocrite, I just want to rid myself of you once and for all." "The more I deny your evil, the smaller you get." "You see spider, I have a choice in the matter...I have a wonderful thing called FREE WILL...I can choose to think any way I like...You can only exist, if I allow you the corner in my mind. You are a cipher...a wisp of air...a lightweight weakling, if I don't allow you to control me."

"Spider, you try to circumvent my good intentions...You are slick." "As long as I hold this pen in my hand, I can control you. The tale of you tempting Jesus in the desert is a good example of our ongoing battle. True heroes face you every day and win most of the battles!"

The spider says, "You don't control anything!" "I will always be here, waiting, lurking, looking for that little chink out of your suit of armor, Mr. Lancelot!" "All it's going to take for your demise, is a lustful smile from some cocktail waitress, or maybe a cold beer on a hot day." "Maybe it will be an argument with your wife or your daughter, that brings you back to me...It will be just like the old days!" "Once I get my fangs into you this next time, you wont have the strength to fight me off anymore." "You will get fat and sick in your old age, from all the wonderful pleasures of my evil!" "You know you want them all, asshole!" "Don't fear the Grim Reaper, we're all going to die anyway!" "Give up, have some fun...Don't be a pussy!"

I say to him, "Spider, I chose life five years ago...I got sober...I was sober for my mother when she died in my arms... I was sober for my brother when he died back in December of last year...I continue to love and remain faithful to my wife...My daughter has regained her love and respect for me... All these gifts come to me from living morally...I am in the hands of God...I haven't given up in the face of adversity...I have overcome illness, alcoholism, and other addictions in my life...I believe in doing the next right thing...As long as I act in accordance with God's will, all will be well." I pray, "Dear Lord, I place myself in your hands to do what you want with me." "I am your servant, a vehicle to do your good." "Please Lord, show me your way."

"You see spider, I put my life in the hands of God...One day at a time!" I pray, "God grant me the serenity, to accept the things I cannot change, the courage to change the things I can, and the wisdom to know the difference."

I watched the spider cower back into his corner. He seemed

devastated by what I had just said to him. He had no reply for me. I felt sorry for him. I forgave him for his evilness. The more compassion I felt for him, the smaller he became, until I could hardly see him anymore...finis.

***

EPILOGUE

As the reader of these selections, you have seen the 'spider' appear in me and my characters many times. At other times we display our humanity, goodness and courage. We humans can be a noble lot...At other times, we are capable of the most monstrous acts. This dichotomy has existed throughout the history of mankind. I suppose that's why there is a war going on in the world somewhere, all the time.

Our salvation lies in our acceptance of basic noble truths, and acting on them. This simple act lifts us to a life of peace and dignity. Every individual in this world has the gift to choose between good and evil. I think on some basic level, we all want to do good. We learn much about ourselves from birth to the grave. What was important to me at the age of thirty, doesn't mean that much to me at the age of fifty-nine. My priorities have changed. I realized I needed to develop my capacity to love. If I have love in my heart, I gain an inner calmness. I get to see reality more clearly. Finding a special calmness takes a lifetime of trial and error. I fail every day in my search, but continue to pick myself up and seek "the good". I try to make my spider smaller every day. Thanks to all of you, who have purchased my first book, "The Journey, Memoirs of a South-Side Chicago kind of guy". You all gave me the impetus and confidence, to try this book-writing adventure, one more time!

***

Remember to love one another!
Sincerely,
Richard J. Cronborg, a human being.

www.ingramcontent.com/pod-product-compliance
Lightning Source LLC
Chambersburg PA
CBHW070840310526
45793CB00010B/28